"Nasrin connects us to the Light through her Spiritual readings with the Ascended Masters. As she echoes the voice of these Beings, she brings us closer to the love and spiritual wellness that we are all seeking. It has been an honor for me to receive this guidance to the Light. She has impacted so many by her sincere effort to open the hearts of humankind."
— Donna Lozito, Animal Communication Specialist

"Thank you for all you have done to make the communication available on the Internet. I have been feeling the shift and try to find out more. I cannot stop crying when I read the messages. Thanks again, I am so grateful for all that you have done."
— J.H., Melbourne Australia

"I am ever so grateful to have been guided to your website. Since my Life Reading, I have new pride in who I am and rejoice in my essence and lineage. Everything good is in my power My heart feels pure."
— J.P., Massachusetts

"There is nothing more inspiring than to know all we do in this life, our joys, our desires, our pain, our cries are heard and felt by those Divine souls that have gone before us. The Divine Masters do take every step with us and wish only to serve us in our journey back to the Divine. Through this book Nasrin gives real, tangible, palpable and above all, beautiful accounts of journeys to the Divine realms with the Masters. I thank Nasrin and the Masters for the joy this book has given me and anyone that is led through grace to it."
— James Foster, AIA, New York NY

"I was just running a Radionic treatment on myself to clear junk from the Thymus Chakra, which has been causing me much psychic pain. Immediately I think of the I AM presence and begin an internet search for some Mantras or invocations. I came across your beautiful, powerful work and am writing to say THANK YOU for being and doing you! I've downloaded some of them, will share some with clients and can feel my vibration rise even as I skim through. Yippee! Thanks for coming, thanks for being a lightworker and thanks for getting your energy and power up and running. Thanks for doing your best to help yourself and the rest of us in this time of need and evolution. Much Love to you.
— Peter T., Holistic Practitioner, Asheville NC

"I attended one of Nasrin's conferences and was impressed by her message and became interested in exploring the topics she discussed more. I decided to schedule a reading with her and was moved by the content of the divine message and information she conveyed. I would highly recommend her to anyone who is looking for spiritual guidance, and I have confidence in her message and the empathy with which it is conveyed."

—A.C. Brown University Rhode Island

Gifts From the Masters of Light

Journeys Into the Inner Realms of Consciousness

by Nasrin Safai
Waves of Bliss Publishing

Gifts III

Cover photo courtesy of NASA/AURA/STSCI Hubble, 2005. Cover design by Karen Bosch, 2005

Gifts From the Masters of Light: Journeys Into the Inner Realms of Consciousness - Gifts III
ISBN 0-9767035-0-5

To order books from Waves of Bliss Publishing:
Email: info@WavesOfBliss.com, Website: www.WavesOfBliss.com

Other books by Nasrn Safai
Gifts From Ascended Beings of Light: Prayers, Meditations, Mantras and Journeys for Soul Growth — Gifts I. Agapi Publishing, 2003.
Gifts of Practical Guidance for Daily Living: Healing, Protection, Manifestation, Enlightenment — Gifts II. Waves of Bliss Publishing, TBA.
Gifts of Wisdom and Truth from the Masters of Light: Tools for Clearing, Release,, Abundance and Empowerment — Gifts IV. Waves of Bliss Publishing. TBA.
Gifts From Sanat Kumara: The Plnetary Logos — Gifts V. Waves of Bliss Publishing. TBA.

Altered States, Biographies & Personal Experience, Body Mind & Spirit, Chakras, Channeling, Consciousness: Awareness & Expansion, Creation Spirituality, Daily Meditation, Everyday Spirituality, God, Meditation & Prayer, New Age, Origin & Destiny of Individual Souls, Science & Religion, Spiritual Teachers, Spirituality, Self Help, The Self

STAR QUEST PUBLISHING
RENO. NV   PHOENIX. AZ
New perspectives in Unified Consciousness.
3030 E. Shangri-La Rd., Phoenix AZ 85028
info@starquestpublishing.com 602-482-1568
www.starquestpublishing.com/index.htm
Printed in China.

Dedicated in the name of the I AM THAT I AM

to Christ Maitreya and Sanat Kumara

in humble gratitude for their presence

through the pages of this book,

and for all the blessings they bestow upon us,

and to Lord Metatron and all the ascended masters

on the path of service to light.

Foreword

by James Foster, American Institute of Architects (AIA)

My search for the truth in this lifetime started when I was a child growing up in the mid-west. This search has continued throughout my life in various settings and circumstances as I experienced different religions and viewpoints on God and Spirituality along the way. One day in October of 2004, it led to an unlikely phone meeting with Nasrin Safai.

I was introduced to Nas by a mutual friend in a seemingly random and accidental way. But as we all know there are no accidents, and that has only become more evident with every passing day since. Although I have known my dear friend Nas for only a short time, we have taken many long voyages together and gone on many adventures similar to those in this amazing book.

This is not just a book to read, this is a book to experience. And the fantastic thing about the presentations in this book is that every person that reads (or rather, experiences) this book will have their own individual and unique experiences as they digest and assimilate what is offered. We all see our reality slightly differently than anyone else, and the exercises in expanding boundaries of reality that this book brings only accents this wonderful truth. The journey from our mundane Americanized reality to the realms of the Ascended Masters and Divine Beings is an abrupt one. That first step takes a leap of faith and an undying need to know who you really are powered by the subtle but never fading need to return to God Unity.

Once the veil is lifted to this broader reality, however, the cork can never be put back on the bottle. You will never see the reality that you are plopped into the middle of in the same way again, and your personal voyage back to the Source will undoubtedly either begin or become more profound. You will also understand why the most common phrase I have repeated to Nasrin over and over again since we began our adventure has been, "...OK, I'm having a little problem getting my arms around that one!" But don't worry; our arms are long enough.

I celebrate the fact that these experiences are made available for all to read. The most amazing gift of all is that there are no two people who will read these books and have exactly the same experience from reading them. We are each individualized sparks of God finding our way home, and each one of us has our very own special way of getting there. Each experience described herein will be different for each of you as you take your very own individual journey along with those being written about. Nobody else could have exactly the same experience because they are not you, and only you will decide how the experience unfolds in your awareness.

Thanks for everything, Nas, and thank you beyond words to the Masters who have given so very, very much to me and to all of humanity. When you read this book your heart will be bursting with joy to see how much we are loved by them. God bless you, and enjoy the ride!

Jim Foster, MA, AIA , July 8 2005, New York City

James Foster is an architect and builder residing in New York City. Born in Iowa, James went to graduate school at Iowa State University and started out practicing architecture throughout the midwest. Jim moved to New York City in 1982 and built a successful architectural practice with a high profile and nationally known clientele, including many fortune 500 companies. Jim switched his focus to construction in 1996 and since then has provided architectural consulting services for a major construction company which completes in excess of $400 Million worth of construction yearly in New York City and across the United States.

Table of Contents

Introduction   1

The Great Invocation   24
Explanation   25

Christ Maitreya   27
Introduction   27
In The Presence of Christ Maitreya   38

Divine Mother   42
Introduction   42
Energies of Divine Mother Pouring Down to Earth   49
Balancing the Male and Female Polarities   51

Elohim of Peace   54
Introduction   54
Elohim of Peace   56

Melchizedek   60
Introduction   60
Protection and Guidance Through the Sphere
of Illumination   61
Manifesting With the Blue Sphere of Illumination   68
Mantra to Bring Forth the Light of Truth Before the
Presence of Christ Maitreya   74

Mother Mary   76
Introduction   76
On Ascension   78
Ascension of Earth   83

Quan Yin   87

Introduction   87

Return of the Kumaras   90

Anchoring the Ray of Remembrance   93

Merging With the Kumara of Your Soul Lineage   95

Journey to Shamballa   97

Orion: Initiation by the Feminine Principle   103

Unlimited Light and Healing for All Kingdoms   105

Visiting Venusian Temples of Wisdom in Dreamtime   109

Minerva   111

Introduction   111

Minerva: Prayers and Journeys   113

Journey to Venus, Orion, Arcturus and Sirius   118

The Mother, Father and Dolphin Child: The Cosmic
Christ Grid   123

Metatron   128

Introduction   128

Golden Sphere of Righteousness, Compassion
and Grace   131

Own Your Divinity Through Commandments
and Decrees   136

Energy Harmonics from Orion to Achieve
Critical Mass   143

Receiving the Original Template and Blueprint For
Your Divine Purpose   145

Receiving a New Contract for Highest Service to
The Light   151

Sanat Kumara Offers Initiation Into Service of
The Light   154

Venus, Home of Shamballa: Journey Through the
Portal of Light   158
Journey to Orion for Light and Compassion   162

Thoth   **167**
Introduction   167
Connection to the Cosmic Sun   173
The Kumara Twin Flames   177
Viewing the Solar System From Space   181
Goddess Venus, The Cosmic Guardian   184
Return To Atlantis — Union With Twin Flame   187

Soul Lineage of Light   **190**
Synopsis   190
Introduction and Invocation   192
The Creation of the Solar System   195
The Seven Mighty Elohim and the Seven Rays   199
The Seven-Fold Flame of the Seven Mighty Elohim   201
The Seven Mighty Elohim Guarding the Seven Rays   202
Golden Ages and the Divine Plan   207

Acknowledgements   **214**

Cited Works   **216**
Information from Organizations or Websites   217

Information on Life Readings   **218**

About The Author   **220**
Other Books by Nasrin Safai   221

What Is Channeling?   **222**

Introduction

The material that is presented here came together in that same magical way that energy always flows when the Masters are directing it...

My dear friend and co-traveler on the path of light Susan took upon herself the task of transcribing the recordings and archiving the readings. This was a major task which over a few months rendered many hundreds of pages of typewritten materials.

When the year 2005 approached, Metatron, my primary guide, who is also known as El Shaddai gave me instructions to put Books II and III of the *Gifts* series together. Metatron advised us to get together in Germany to go over the transcripts in the divine grace energies of a living saint who makes her home there. Mother Meera, the essence of the energies of Divine Mother, is an avatar, an enlightened soul who has fully awakened the divine spark within her and attained full mastery. She is beyond the precepts of the law of karma and has no need of incarnation on Earth.

In her love for the light and to bring that light to Earth, she has taken yet another human incarnation to save the souls of her devotees and to bring the light of the Paramatman to Earth. Para means beyond and Atman is the self. When the soul realizes the self, it becomes the Atman. Para-ma-Atman is that which lies beyond the Atman, the pure light without differentiation. Mother Meera resides in Germany and, together with her most devoted disciple Adilakshmi, she receives hundreds of devotees from all over the world.

Susan and I began the work on the transcripts of the discourses for the books in Germany. Once we had a sense of what we were to do and had received the graceful blessing of Mother Meera, we headed home, Susan to the west coast and I to the east coast and the south. Metatron next instructed us to bring the first draft with us to India. We were to perform ceremonies for the entry to the thousand years of peace on March Equinox of 2005.

When I sat down to work on the second phase of the project, I began to feel completely overwhelmed. I was trying to adjust to the heightened energies of the Equinox and the heat of India. While my head was hot and heavy, I struggled to get into my mind to no avail. That was when the magic of the guidance from on high came to the rescue. I heard Lord Metatron's voice say, "Don't panic, you don't have to read through everything before you can divide them. Sit still and thumb through each transcript. I will tell you where it belongs." I did, and in minutes I had three piles in front of me: a Book II pile, a Book III pile and a Hold pile. I didn't know then that he was planning three books altogether. He was holding back, concerned that the prospect of working on three books all at once would throw me for a loop!

When I presented the piles to Susan, she looked through the piles and said, "Funny, how I had filed the transcripts in the same order!" Many phases of fantastic coincidences coupled with the churning of the stomach, stilling the mind and surrender to the divine have ensued. The outcome has borne fruit in the book you hold in your hand.

There are two strong themes that weave a tapestry of light through the pages of this book. The first one is the presence of Christ Maitreya who is our World Teacher and who is presently in physical embodiment awaiting the call from the yearning hearts of the multitudes and masses of humanity to make his presence known to the world. He is here out of his love for humanity and to serve the light. He is here to bring us the truth of our divinity. He is here most importantly to tilt the balance of dark and light in favor of the light and to take us to our home, our ultimate destination: God unity.

Benjamin Crème, the founder of Share International Foundation (www.shareintl.org) and the spokesperson for the Masters of Wisdom who represent the energies of Christ Maitreya, writes in his book *Maitreya's Mission*:

" We are entering the 'crisis of love.' This is the experience which the human race faces as it enters that period in its evolutionary journey when it will, as a whole, demonstrate the quality of love and take its place in the kingdom of souls, the esoteric hierarchy. During the Aquarian Age, the aim of the Christ Maitreya, the hierophant, will be to initiate millions of people, in group formation, into the hierarchy. Eventually, by the end of the age, the vast majority of humanity will have taken their places in the spiritual kingdom, the esoteric hierarchy, at some stage or other. Vast numbers will take the first and some will take the second initiation.

This is an extraordinary event to be happening on a mass scale. It shows the success of the evolutionary plan as it is envisaged by the Lord of the World, Sanat Kumara, on Shamballa, and carried out by his agents, the planetary hierarchy." (volume 1, pp.154-5)

In another message Crème states,
*"The Christ Maitreya, is the Hierophant at the first and second initiations and the third and higher initiations being taken before the Lord of the World, Sanat Kumara at Sham-balla." (*Maitreya's Mission, *volume 1, p.174)*

Sanat Kumara is the second theme which weaves its golden light through the tapestry of this book. Sanat Kumara is our planetary logos, or the "word" for our planet. (In the beginning was the Word, and the Word was with God and the Word was God. John 1:1.) His word is the life giving force which keeps all the souls on the planet away from harm and extinction. It is because of him that the life force on the planet bears the consciousness of light and shall remain to see the dawning of the seventh golden age, the Age of Aquarius. In a channeled book by Alice A. Bailey, called *Initiations Human and Solar*, Master Djwal Khul (known also as the Tibetan) p. 28, says,
"In the middle of the Lemurian epoch, approximately 18,000,000 years ago, occurred a great event which signified the following development — the planetary logos of our Earth scheme, one of the seven spirits before the throne (of God) took physical incarnation and, under the form of Sanat Kumara, the Ancient of Days, and the Lord of the

world, came down to this dense physical plane and has remained with us ever since." He then goes on to say that because Sanat Kumara's nature was pure, he could not take a dense physical body but functions in his etheric body. This body however, is so vast and so strong that the entire Earth is held inside its radius. He left the high lofty places of glory and light to come to the density of Earthly planes to help the evolution of humankind. Sanat Kumara resides in the Palace of Shamballa in Venus. He has been waiting for the time when the quotient of light on our planet and in the hearts of humankind is raised to such high levels where he can walk on Earth again. And that time is here, now. "

Janet McClure, in her book *The Story of Sanat Kumara-Training a Planetary Logos*, gives an account of Sanat Kumara's training; the gist of the sweet and compelling story is this: to become qualified for his position as the planetary logos, Sanat Kumara had to divide his consciousness into a circle containing 900,000 pieces of his soul. Each piece had to then incarnate in a planet in the galaxy and serve until it accomplished its mission through raising the consciousness of the planet and all the souls. Then each piece of his soul could return to the circle and merge as one. As more of his soul's pieces gained enlightenment and returned to the circle, an awareness of all his pieces formed. The ultimate exercise was to be fully aware of the condition of each of the 900,000 pieces. To accomplish this he went for training to Venus, our sister planet where in the Temples of Wisdom he trained under supervision of great cosmic beings of light.

Adonis, his teacher, was one such being and Venus, the deity of the planet Venus was another. This book is written with great simplicity to explain the magnitude of the service of our planetary logos and the caliber of his great essence. Master Vywamus, who has channeled this information to Janet McClure, is himself a great cosmic being. He has stated through other sources that he could clear the entire beingness of our planet and restore her to the pristine original intent in a matter of fifteen minutes by putting his focus on it. However, he has also said that he would be depriving humankind from learning a great lesson if he did that.

The many Masters who speak to us through the pages of this book are all in celebration of this fact. They have hand-picked their favorite journeys, meditations, healings and initiations to anchor the energies of Shamballa (heaven) back here on Earth — where it belongs — and to ensure that the return of the planetary Logos Sanat Kumara is felt and experienced consciously in the DNA structure of all those who read these pages. This indeed is yet another gift from the Masters of Light and Wisdom to us.

We begin our journey with the Prayer of Great Invocation, calling upon the Masters of Wisdom and Christ Maitreya to start the transmission of higher vibrational energies. Melchizedek weaves the truth into a simple but potent mantra filling it inside his sphere of illumination in the presence of Christ Maitreya. Metatron, Quan Yin, Thoth and Minerva, the Elohim of Illumination, each take great pleasure in bringing us for initiations in the presence of Sanat Kumara from the Palace of Shamballa in Venus through exotic journeys to Orion, Arcturus, Sirius, out of the solar system into the galaxy, the universe, the Cosmos and the

Great Central Sun of the Cosmic Conglomerate. Along the path of soul growth we receive the blessing of Alpha and Omega, the deities of the great central sun, to ensure our speedy evolution to higher light and the much-needed spiritual growth, which can warrant us a discipleship to the Masters and grant us the opportunity to serve the light at this prime juncture of events in the evolution of our entire universe.

Furthering our understanding of spiritual evolution and the path of initiation through the wise words of our beloved Mother Mary, we have a better grasp of the process of and the steps leading to Ascension, personal and planetary. She assimilates the stages of evolution from awakening to full Mastery and Ascension to the birth of a new born baby and the various stages of growth to full adulthood. Mother Mary explains that what is misconstrued for ascension is in fact different levels of initiation from spiritual awakening to attainment of full mastery. To clarify these levels, I will briefly give an overview.

The stages of initiation leading to full Ascension begin at the first level of initiation which requires the control of the physical body and its physical needs, urges and desires. This first level is in fact the state of awakening, the very first step in the direction of spiritual evolution.

The second initiation requires of the initiate to build control over the emotional body, which means harnessing the highs and lows of emotions. The second level initiate is capable of living life from a neutral position where the personality bears witness to the events rather than drowning itself in the drama of everyday life. This is the most difficult of all the initiations, as emotions are not easily harnessed and attachments to them are difficult to release.

The third initiation is an initiation of the soul aspect — called transfiguration by the esoteric literature. It manifests through control of the mental body and the urges and desires of the mind, contact with the Masters and spirit guides and energy exchange with the esoteric realms takes place at this level of initiation.

The fourth initiation is the renunciation phase of evolution of the soul. In this phase, the initiate lives life in the way that Master Jesus suggested: "Be in the world and not of it." This initiation was the crux of the life of the Master himself as it culminated in his body on the cross of the crucifixion. It is in essence the total act of renunciation, where all is offered in pursuit of Mastery. Worldly possessions, titles and positions, family members, attachments of all kinds, even to life itself are renounced and put to test at this level. The body has become purified to seventy-five percent or more light at this point, making room for the divine light of God unity to enter and merge.

The fifth initiation is the process whereby the initiate has purified itself at all levels of beingness to reach one hundred percent pure light. This phase in the life of Master Jesus was symbolized by resurrection. The initiate vibrating one hundred percent light is no longer bound by matter and it has no need of a physical body. It is at this level of initiation that a Master no longer needs to be born in human physical embodiment, and the wheel of karma and incarnation can stop. The Master is now a perfected Master free from the Earth and its pull.

Ascension is the sixth level of initiation where the perfected Master who is no longer bound by the Earth chooses a life of service, to rescue and initiate those who are bound by Earth or other planetary bodies. The Master attains total immortality and connects to consciousness at cosmic levels. Cosmic beings or great beings which we will journey with through many of the meditations in this book are of that caliber of consciousness. An initiation is an ancient ritual which provides a rite of passage. Mostly a scientific technique (although it may not seem so when reading through the pages of initiatory journeys in this book), it provides a speeding up of the process of the evolution of soul on its journey of discovering its divine origin and divine purpose.

The initiation itself, although marking an achievement of a higher level of evolution, does not warrant maintenance and continuity on the path. What brings continuity is when the initiate seriously pursues higher levels of light and is willing to be tested. Then the initiate becomes, as Metatron would say, "brandished, stainless steel" in strength, stamina and willfulness to evolve and master body, emotions, mind and soul. Finally the initiate finds the spirit of God unity and unites with the universal consciousness in oneness.

To read more specifically about the initiations and the full processes, refer to Alice Bailey's books, *Initiations Human and Solar* and *Rays and Initiations: A Treatise on the Seven Rays*. Alice Bailey was a world-renouned channel from the early and mid 1900's. She channeled a very highly evolved Tibetan Master by the name of Djwal Khul who brought a very large body of information to Earth through her. The Mantra for Great Invocation is attributed

9

to Master Djwal Khul and is seen in the materials from Alice Bailey. The instruction is to have the great invocation freely distributed to humankind as it does not belong to one Master or their disciples but to the world. And its impact is to move the consciousness of humankind through levels of initiation to attainment of Mastery and the final goal of God unity. I have printed the Great Invocation at the beginning of the first chapter of this book on Christ Maitreya. Christ Maitreya, the World Teacher and the leader of the hierarchy has requested the repetition of the Great Invocation by the multitudes and masses.

Benjamin Crème gives complete instructions for the repetition of the Great Invocation in his book, *Transmission*. In it he explains that repetition of the Great Invocation is an invitation to the Masters of Wisdom, who work with Christ Maitreya and Maitreya himself, to begin transmission of energies of light and Mastery to each individual recipient according to their individual needs. The transmission of energies after each repetition of the mantra will continue for as long as necessary for that individual.

In the course of these journeys you may be asked by the Masters to offer a prayer and pause to meditate on your prayers. The Masters' expression of prayer is not begging or supplication. The energy of supplication is concentrated in the solar plexus, and it can make your stomach churn. The intention is to have a heart to heart with the divine. A prayer, as I understand it and as I have always applied it, is a communion with that divine source of which I am a divine spark, and so are you. In fact, many times when someone is receiving their first private channeling session or life reading with me, I tell them this is an interactive session.

Imagine that you have been invited to have tea with friends, except the friend who is sitting across the table from you is Quan Yin or Archangel Michael, or even Metatron. The energy of the prayer which we are referring to is not concentrated in the solar plexus but in the heart. The idea is not that you are powerless or that you need to pray to take the power back, but to let go and let God. This energy is concentrated in the center of the heart.

If prayer is having a heart to heart with the higher powers, meditation is listening intently for their advice. Meditation is moving into that still place in the center of the heart where the mind has no access or permission to enter. All the golden doorways of trust and surrender are open, the walls are down and we are ready and willing not only to listen but to surrender. Through surrender we are able to let go and let God. Through surrender we allow ourselves to give up our free will, to be free from this wonderful free will which the Masters so respectfully observe and which has caused us great pain and forgetfulness of our own origin and our divinity. We can surrender the free will and align our will with the will of the I Am, we can offer it to the Masters or to our own Higher Self — which is our soul self. Then we can live life in non-doership, stop blaming and criticizing ourselves at every bend of the corner, wasting time and energies on all the should have nots which have been and gone awry! Then in surrender we begin each day with, "I offer this day to the I AM THAT I AM," and "I align my will with the will of God, Great Spirit, Ascended Masters, Allah, or I AM," or whatever feels right in your heart and soul.

All of this will happen when we are willing to surrender. Surrender comes when we pause to be still. Call that stillness meditation. Do it on a regular basis, and you can conquer the world with it. The peace and harmony is instilled within your beingness. As that stillness becomes a friend and ally, a regular visitor, the Master's guidance in the form of visual perception and/or verbal communication begins to pour in. That is when the inner realms become perceptible and living in the inner realm becomes exciting. That is when being in the company of the saints who are present in the inner realms with their teachings and their love becomes a greater attraction than anything anyone can offer you in the outside world, the world of mundane level existence.

When people ask me questions like, "But what do you do when you are in silence for so long, how do you entertain yourself? Don't you get bored?" I think to myself, "If only they could see how busy I am receiving guidance and how much more entertaining this inner world is, then they would want to be in on it!" So many times I have said to people, "If you could have a television camera inside of my mind and see what I can see, you would never want to come back to the mundane level, ever again." It is so supernatural and colorful that the greatest panoramic movies ever made pale before it. This is the world that can open up to you for the asking.

When the Masters offer us an invocation or a mantra to repeat, their purpose is to guide us along the path to faster spiritual growth in less time. Repetition of mantras, which are usually sacred syllables of sound, is a tool to speed up the process. The mantras that the Masters offer us through the channelings in these books are not short syllables of sound but long rhythmic sentences, whose power although held in the words is mostly in the contents and the intention for which the long mantras and invocations are given to us. The Masters of Wisdom and the Ascended Masters of Light bring through these invocations and mantras and charge them with the intentions and the power of higher light. The repetition of these sacred texts help to release our obstacles on the path of spiritual evolution and through us spread the energy to others, through the Earth and beyond. These invocations are not only sacred but are also conscious energy fields. As you connect with these energies, something inside of yourself and your own consciousness shifts. And that shift is exactly what the Masters are waiting for. Their hope and desire is that through the repetition of these mantras and invocations we signal to them our willingness to take one step in their direction. They, in turn, take ten steps in our direction.

And that is only the beginning! It is the beginning of a great joint venture which becomes more and more exciting as we grow and as they get closer to us. There comes a time when you wouldn't want to be without them, because the world of the mundane becomes uneventful and boring, and their world is a full-color spectrum of light. Lucky are those who are able to live in this world and not be of it, but of the worlds of higher realms of consciousness, tending the realms of light with both feet firmly on the ground. As our beloved Metatron would remind us time and time again, simply spiritizing matter will no longer be sufficient; during this next golden age we have come together to not only spiritize matter but also materialize spirit. Metatron validates that statement by reminding us that in every successful golden age humanity came to Earth and at best spiritized matter, meaning took the matter of this world, especially this body, blew the breath of spirit into it, purified it, raised its vibration to such high degrees that the matter then became spirit itself and left the body of matter, be it the physical human body or the physical body of the planet, our Mother Earth. Well, what happened next?

Next, those elevated spirits who worked so hard during the last round to free themselves from the matter looked back, saw the matter suspended in air in agony and misery. Out of their compassion they then chose to come back to do it all over again. Now Metatron says we must materialize spirit alongside of spiritizing matter. In this way, we don't have to run off to some exotic fifth-dimensional realm of reality somewhere out there. But we will materialize the spirit and bring the essence of that reality right here on Earth. Then no one has to leave nor does anyone have to sacrifice their heaven to come back to Earth on another rescue mission. Then and only then can we have heaven on Earth.

We can have our cake and eat it because as soon as we are hungry, the cake appears. That would be heaven on Earth! That is what we can expect the fifth-dimensional realms to be like. Instant manifestation is one of the qualities of the fifth dimensional realm. When we raise the vibration of the third-dimension by materializing spirit, those qualities can be manifest right here.

When the Masters talk about decrees and commands, they are urging us to leave our little "poor me" selves behind and become the Masters-in-making which is our divine right and from that divine space to send our decrees, commands and demands to the universe. As a spark of the divine we absolutely can, and we must demand our divine heritage from the universe. And until we demand it, it will not be placed on a golden platter, nor even a silver one to be given to us. We only receive what we believe we are worthy of receiving. And for as long as we believe that we are not worth it, the universe will make no attempt to give us something that even we can not believe we deserve. Only when we have convinced ourselves that we are worth it can we then demand it from the universe. Until then the universe will not respond.

The response to supplication is what? Distaste, perhaps. What happens when your pet begs for food? Generally you raise your voice or hold your hand out and say, "no." How do you respond when you see an able-bodied person begging in the street? Not with great respect, but with compassion perhaps. What happens when that pet barks or meows with great fervor? You respond differently. What happens when that able-bodied person stands in a line at the employment office and demands a job? How would you respond? With compassion, certainly, but also with respect.

The universe responds to open demands and commands. The energy is focused, the will is in charge, the decree is sent out, the command is issued. There is no uncertainty in a decree, a demand or a command as long as it is in the light, in the highest wisdom of the applicant and intends no harm to people, places or things. The universe not only respects it, it also responds to it. The universe gives you your demand or command's worth to the full.

The question is: are you ready to demand it? Are you mature enough to know your own worth and willing to take responsibility for receiving your command's worth?

When the Masters encourage us to command the universe to give us our divine heritage, they are not asking us to be rude or arrogant or selfish or disrespectful. They are asking us to own the reality that we are also sparks of God and that as God-sparks it is our divine right and our heritage to command the universe to bring us the light, the abundance, the spiritual evolution and growth which was and still is ours. We are only demanding what was ours in the first place and are reminding ourselves and the universe that we know it.

With that remembrance comes the responsibility. When you command the universe to spread its light over you, then you are responsible to disperse that light in a manner representative of your divine heritage and according to the will of the divine God-spark. That means you can't act in your own self-interest any more, but in the interest of all creation. That means you can't act irresponsibly any more but must take responsibility for your actions. That means ignorance is no longer bliss and pleading ignorance will not get you off the hook. Most importantly, that means that the divine will must be observed and be regarded as a priority superceding our own free will and our personal desires. That means realigning our will, our little wills, with the great will that is the divine will.

When we understand these precepts, we can function in the realms of reality where our ascended brothers and sisters walk and be taken seriously by them. For as long as we act like pubescent, adolescent teenagers, we have no place in their realms, nor can we expect to be taken seriously. When we take responsibility for our actions and demand from the universe to take us seriously and consistently abide by the universal laws of service (not self-service) and divine love (not selfish, controlling love), then we have earned the merit to walk with our brothers and sisters of light, the Masters.

As you read through the chapters of this book, please pay attention to the following:

- Notice that a Master may give an exercise such as a grid, a meditation or a journey. They may begin the meditation or exercise, and then go off on a tangent, giving a discourse on something directly related or totally unrelated. Then they come back and resume the exercise, meditation or journey. This pattern may be repeated more than once in the course of an excrcise.

I asked Metatron why this was the case. I explained that it was very confusing when they jump from one subject to another, leaving the actual exercise incomplete and returning back to it when we have almost forgotten what we had begun. I asked if it would be more productive that the Masters start with a subject and finish it and then give us the relevant or not-so-relevant discourses.

His response was that it was necessary to work in this format. He said, "When the Masters begin an exercise, they bring down the energy which needs to be anchored in the recipient's body, through the elements, to the Earth and all the multitudes and masses. To complete this task, the mind needs to be out of the way. Especially in the case of people who have extra active minds and are incapable of being still during the course of the meditation. When we give the related or unrelated discourses, the mind gives attention to what we are saying and not what we are doing.

The ego is connected to the mind. When the mind is doing something, the ego sits quietly, watching the mind which is listening to the discourse. The ego is not threatened, therefore it does not have a need to jump in and distract the mind. The idea is to get the ego out of the way and occupy the mind so the energies can be anchored by the Masters without the interference of the ego. Through the course of the time required to anchor these energies, we give you very important and effective information for the mind to absorb and utilize. In the case of those few whose ego is harnessed and who are capable of stilling their mind, these exercises are given without discourses, but with long pauses and moments of stillness in between each segment of the exercise. The information in the discourse is given elsewhere. Time is needed, however, for the anchoring of the energies whether we talk to you through the exercises or have you sit still and receive it."

- It is important that you not concern yourself with doing the exercise, meditation or journey "right" but that you sidestep the mind and put forth a pure intention. Free yourself from judgment and expectation, and just relax and experience. Although an exercise, meditation or journey presented in a somewhat circuitous manner may be an irritant to the linear mind that always wants things in order, there is something to be learned and experienced here. Trust the process. Metatron has told us, "We are repetitive. We know we are repetitive. Do not edit!"

- Be patient through these exercises, and if you desire to repeat them, learn them by heart or write down the steps. Do them step by step with pauses in between. And give yourself time to recover and return to your normal state of consciousness after each exercise, because you may enter into altered states of consciousness during the exercises. It may be helpful to journal your experiences immediately after you have finished to help you process and to ground you back into your daily life.

- Remember that the information that is contained in this book was given over a span of three years to more than one person. This material needs to be processed by your body and your being over time. I do appreciate and hope that the information piques your interest to the point where you can't put it down. Nevertheless, I ask that you heed the needs of your body as it processes the information in its own time. The examples below may shed some light on this:

When I sent the manuscript to my friend Toni Maria for proofreading and critique, we agreed that she would give me an overview within ten days, as I was about to leave for my second trip to Germany to see Mother Meera since taking up this project. The morning of departure she called me and said, "Normally, I would have easily finished this draft by now. However, I have been sitting behind my computer reading a journey or meditation. My mind becomes still, my heart starts pulsing, my hands and feet begin to tingle and I am off orbiting some planet or constellation in an altered state of consciousness. Then I come back to normal consciousness and realize that a heap of time has passed. My mind is foggy and I need to take a nap before I can function again. Suffice it to say, that I have only covered one-third of the book." And then she added, "The good news is that everything that the Masters mentioned has happened in my body and I have felt it." I laughed long and hard and told her that if the review has merely achieved that, it has been worthwhile.

- If you don't feel tingly or feel sleepy, it doesn't mean you haven't received any benefit. It simply means you have received and absorbed at your own pace, according to your needs as the Masters see fit to administer to you. Some people have great, tangible experiences and some people have very subtle experiences, but everyone receives. Whether you feel the impact of these exercises, meditations and journeys or not, things do happen to you at different levels of consciousness. If you don't feel the energy move through you, it doesn't mean it hasn't. The conscious awareness happens over time, and even then you may not realize that the trigger for what has happened to you was reading the book. Again, journaling is a helpful way to process and follow your own progress through these experiences and may bring wonderful new insights.
- Remember to take your time with the book if necessary. One young indigo adult (souls of the seventh ray who are extremely sensitive to heightened energies) professed that she felt so much love coming from the Masters' words in the first *Gifts* book (*Gifts from Ascended Beings of Light*) that she could only

read a small portion at a time. She had to leave the book, process it all and come back for more later.

- The opposite of that is also true. Many have relayed to me that they felt the love of the Masters and did not want to put the book down. The divine energy of the Masters and the divine power of the words move each person in the exact manner that is specific and unique for each individual. What may work for others, may not work for you. Trust the process.

- When you begin a journey, it is best to read through all the segments to the end before you put the book down. For the greater ease in reading, I have divided the journeys into segments with different topics. The entire journey, however, is one reading, as you can tell by the dates. It should be completed in one sitting. In effect, part of your essence needs to go on the journey and come back when it is complete, according to the instructions of the Master who is taking you on this journey.

- If you are interrupted in your reading and must return to normal consciousness quickly, it is not the end of the world. You may feel out of sorts for a while or experience that your energy is bouncing all over the place, somewhat like a bumpy landing in an aircraft. To remedy that, when you become conscious of this feeling, call upon the Masters and simply say,

"I ask the Masters of Light for a recalibration of my body, mind, emotions, soul and spirit to return to normal consciousness, in the name of the "I AM THAT I AM."

The intention is what is important rather than the exact sequence of the words. What is important is to remember to qualify every intent in the name of the I AM THAT I AM. The I AM THAT I AM is the energy and essence of God in form, the highest and the most potent of the God vibration which you can call to your assistance. Anything that is asked in the name of the "I AM THAT I AM" is, by the universal law, dispensed to you if it is your highest wisdom and does not cause or intend harm. No energy or force can interfere or pollute, divert or delay the dispensation that is issued from that level of God vibration, the vibration of the I AM THAT I AM.

If you remember this and start each day by invoking the I Am Presence, you will receive the presence and protection throughout the day. You may end each day with the same invocation and receive the guidance and protection throughout the night. All you need to say is, "I offer this day to The Presence of The I AM THAT I AM." "I offer this night to The Presence of The I AM THAT I AM." The presence of God in form will imbue everything around you and within you in God vibration and keep you safe in its own divinity and its light.

- Reading through the chapters of this book you will come across many new terminologies, names, exercises and beings that may be unknown to you. Please persevere and continue to read as this material is charged by the Masters of Light. Even though you may think you're not fully comprehending everything in the book, you receive the energy. The seed is planted which will bear fruit in time. Even when the mind is incapable of digesting the information the heart can absorb the energies and in time the heart and the mind will align and you will have great results. This book is like a seed that the Masters plant in the heart, while the mind is impatient to see the fruits, the heart can bathe in the love and nurturance which vibrates from the seed. It will eventually bear fruit. Your mind will be at peace and your Self — your God Self — will be elated for the connection that is finally made between it and your consciousness. The Masters of Light, especially Christ Maitreya and Sanat Kumara have brought this information to Earth to jump-start all of you who read it to higher levels of initiation. You may be a high level initiate and not consciously know it. Once you are connected to the energies of Christ Maitreya and Sanat Kumara through this book, you will begin to remember. Then you will recall ways to connect with them directly, and receive your own guidance. You will also be able to assist them with the Divine Plan as it is unfolding before our eyes. That alone would be a worthwhile plan to undertake. To the masters presented in this book, I offer prayers for the success of your endeavor in attaining greater initiations through light and discipleship.

Thank you very much for your attention to the above. May all your journeys be on the path of Light, led by the Masters of Light, and in the love of the I AM THAT I AM.

The Great Invocation

From the point of light within the mind of God

Let light stream forth into the minds of men.

Let Light descend on Earth.

From the point of love within the Heart of God

Let love stream forth into the hearts of men.

May Christ return to Earth.

From the center where the Will of God is known

Let purpose guide the little wills of men —

The purpose which the Masters know and serve.

From the center which we call the race of men

Let the plan of love and light work out

And may it seal the door where evil dwells.

Let light and love and power

Restore the plan on Earth.

Explanation

The Prayer of the Great Invocation has been around for many decades. It was given by Master Djwal Khul to Alice Bailey and was first introduced to the world in June 1945 at the close of World War II. It was brought to Earth by the Masters of Wisdom to raise the vibration of Earth and all souls. Christ Maitreya imbued the Great Invocation with his own energy. He recites daily the higher dimensional energetic version of this invocation in sacred language of light. He has also instructed the Masters of Wisdom to offer the prayer together with the transmission of higher vibrational energies from the realms of the Ascended Masters to humankind.

To connect with his energy, it is important that we recite the exact words of the Great Invocation as it was given to humankind by the Masters without any change or modification to the text. The true language of this prayer is the language of light. When we recite The Great Invocation we connect to the sacred language of light and the Masters who recite it daily, and we receive the shower of their blessings transmitted to us throughout our day. Repeated recitation magnifies the impact.

Transmission meditation, which has been popularized by Benjamin Crème in his teachings at various workshops and published books, is now practiced throughout the world. Groups of people gather together or simply make an agreement to say the Prayer of Invocation daily and to connect to the Masters of Wisdom through the recitation of the prayer, receiving the transmission of the higher energies from the Masters of Wisdom under the leadership of Christ Maitreya.

To accelerate your spiritual growth and to strengthen your connection with the Masters of Wisdom, recite the Great Invocation daily with great love and sincerity. And invoke the Masters of Wisdom and Christ Maitreya to begin the transmission of the higher energies to you. You may sit in meditation if you so choose. The transmission will begin as you recite The Great Invocation each day and will continue for as many hours as you need it, whether you are focused on the Masters and in meditation or not. The length of the transmission is unique to each individual recipient. The Masters of Wisdom will give each person the exact amount of energy and light that their consciousness can bear to hold at each recitation.

I have recited The Great Invocation in times where I have desired to accelerate my own pace of spiritual growth, daily with every breath, for as long as I could keep my mind focused on it. The life changes that I have experienced are enormous, both in my inner consciousness and in my outer life. I don't know any other prayer, invocation, decree, command, tool or technique that is more effective at this present moment of Earth's history. The acceleration pace of The Great Invocation is parallel to none.

Christ Maitreya

Introduction

Christ Maitreya is our World Teacher and the leader of the Masters of Wisdom and their disciples. He is the planetary Christ in that he carries the consciousness of the Christed self, or the true Self — the enlightened Self. His presence on Earth at this juncture of Earth's evolution is to assist the Masters of Light to bring their disciples, those who have already awakened to their divinity, to Mastery and to awaken the spiritually unawakened souls to the consciousness of the divine spark.

At this present moment, the Earth is populated by a very large majority of unawakened souls (more than 99%). It is the hope of Christ Maitreya and the Masters of Wisdom to bring one percent of the population of Earth to receive their first level of initiation, which is awakening to the divine spark within. It is foreseen that critical mass can be achieved at one percent to trigger the awakening of the multitudes and masses. This will also trigger those who have attained the first level of initiation to move through the second level of initiation, as I have explained in the introduction. The critical mass for the second level of initiation is one-tenth of one percent of the population of Earth.

Those of you who are holding this book in your hand are at least in this category of spiritual evolution. You would not have been drawn to this book and the energies of the Masters otherwise. Christ Maitreya is physically present on Earth to bring forth the manifestation of this great feat for the present civilization of Earth. Christ Maitreya's mission is to accelerate these two levels of initiation for the multitudes and masses. And to push those who have already attained these levels to their next spiritual attainment, the third and fourth levels of initiation, and entry into realms of Mastery.

At the first and second levels of initiation, humanity is awakening to its own divinity, realizing two very important factors in connecting with one's own soul and spirit.
1. "I am not this body, therefore I am not bound by the limitations of this body. "
2. "I am not these emotions, therefore, I am not bound by the limitations of these emotions."
As the World Teacher, this is the greatest and the most important of the teachings that he has brought to Earth.

Many religions of the Earth have professed to the return of the World Teacher, calling him by different names relevant to each faith. The Buddhists are awaiting the return of Maitreya Buddha, the Buddha yet to come. The Muslims are awaiting the return of Imam Mahdi, the messenger who is the knower of truth, the revealer of knowledge. The Jews are awaiting the return of the Messiah. The Hindus are expecting the return of Krishna. The Christians are ready for the second coming of the Christ. The Zoroastrians, return of the light of the sun, the son of Zarathustra. And the Bahai, the return of the glory of the light of God. All other faiths in one form or another are expecting peace and harmony to return to Earth through the second coming of the light of God. All peoples of faith are expecting his return.

Christ Maitreya is the title of the office that he holds, the office of the World Teacher. He holds the energies of the Christed self, the consciousness of which was brought down to Earth through the energies of divine love. Master Jesus anchored the divine love energies on Earth in his lifetime as Jeshua ben Joseph, Jesus the son of Joseph through the sacrifice he made upon his crucifixion and resurrection.

Christ Maitreya, the being who resided in the office of the World Teacher during the life of Jesus, was the guiding force and the Master light that gave of his own divine light for the life, the crucifixion and the resurrection energies to be anchored on Earth through Jesus the man. In his life as Jesus the man, he was a third level initiate, a disciple of Christ Maitreya. In his crucifixion, he renounced the world and attained the fourth level of initiation, becoming the Master who is no longer bound by the limitations of Earth and the karma of earthly entanglements in the wheel of birth and death. In his resurrection, he entered as an initiate of fifth level Mastery, where he was no longer bound by a physical body of matter and could manifest the etheric body of light to complete his mission of service. Once the soul that we know as Jesus graduated from his fifth level of initiation, he became an Ascended Master. At that point he attained the title of Chohan of the sixth ray, the Ray of Universal Brotherhood and Sisterhood of Service and the Peace of God. After many centuries of service, Ascended Master Jesus graduated from the office of Chohan of the sixth ray to that of the World Teacher. He held the office of World Teacher with Master Kuthumi who was the Chohan of the second ray, the Ray of Illumination and the Wisdom of God. These two Ascended Masters together moved up to hold the office of World Teacher, freeing Christ Maitreya from

29

his responsibilities as the World Teacher. (This sequence of events took place in the mid-1950's. (For more information, see the chapter on Soul Lineage of Light.)

Christ Maitreya chose to return to Earth to assist all souls to awaken to their spirituality and reach first and second levels of initiation. This event is happening right now. He will assist those who have already attained first and second levels to move to higher levels. Christ Maitreya works with Sanat Kumara, our planetary logos. It is to him that Christ Maitreya brings the initiates who are about to attain their third level of initiation. Once they receive their third level of initiation, they are connected with the energies of Sanat Kumara.

Christ Maitreya instructed me to make his energies available in this book. The objective is to help the first and second level initiates become consciously aware of his presence and invoke his guidance in all walks of life. Also to create a bridge from Christ Maitreya to Sanat Kumara where third and forth level initiates can connect, at much greater and deeper levels, consciously to the planetary Logos. The spiritual evolution of the high level initiates can be accelerated enormously once this connection is made. Until then, attainment of full mastery is halted. A full master is bound to have made contact with the planetary Logos for this final phase. The initiate, as highly evolved as she/he may be, cannot attain full mastery without training under the planetary Logos.

The attainment of full mastery is halted pending this final phase. Once the connection is made, the scope is no longer limited. The opportunities expand to service at global and interplanetary levels. I have come across very frustrated and unhappy 4th-level initiates who found true bliss once they connected with Sanat Kumara. The lonely heart and joyless life gave way to great leaps to action in service of the beloved Logos and the Masters of Light. The scriptures say that in the age of Kali Yuga (where we are now in the evolution of Earth) simply remembering the "Word" will bring you to self-realization. The "Word" is the planetary Logos, Sanat Kumara.

It is a pleasant surprise and a great gift to both Susan and I to present this material to you. In the process, we have grown leaps and bounds in our own spiritual growth and in appreciation of the energies that move through us by the grace of the Masters presented in this book and the honor of working directly with Sanat Kumara and Christ Maitreya.

I first heard of Christ Maitreya in the early 1990's while attending a four day angel workshop in the Blue Ridge mountain area of Virginia. After each day ended, groups of participants would sit at dinner together discussing various spiritual subjects. In these types of settings, one can learn great beneficial information to equal and sometimes surpass the content of the workshop itself. One such subject was the return of the Christ Maitreya to Earth. I listened intently to the information that was given and felt the vibration of the energy as the conversation moved around the table, with each group member adding their own bit to the pile.

I heard that Christ Maitreya as the World Teacher had chosen to walk on Earth to bring higher light to humankind. He is the one who taught Jeshua ben Joseph, or Jesus son of Joseph and Mary, the higher spiritual wisdom and the potent words and parables which he relayed to humankind. Another added that he is the long-awaited Imam Mahdi whose return to Earth is expected by those of the Muslim faith as the final and greatest messenger of God. One said he lived in the Middle East and had recently moved to the west residing somewhere in Europe, but he manifests at will wherever he wishes to appear and gives his blessings to all present. Another talked of the crosses of light that are mysteriously appearing on walls and windows of people's homes, water wells which have magical healing powers and statues of Mother Mary that cry tears of blood. They claimed that these were all acts of Christ Maitreya who has promised to manifest many more miracles, including a total of 777 healing water sources all around the world.

As people talked, I listened and prayed that if indeed, such a man existed, I want to know about him. Furthermore, I want to be in his presence—his physical presence.

That night, I lay in bed in my hotel room and began to pray and meditate. Remembering the stories of the evening, I called out that name Christ Maitreya and said, "Master, if you are here on Earth, I would like to be in your presence. Universe, if there is such a being available to Earth, I want to know him." My prayers became more fervent, and the heat began to build around me as I repeated my desire to know and be in the presence of Christ Maitreya. Suddenly, I felt my consciousness pulled out of my body, and I experienced myself kneeling at the feet of Christ Maitreya who appeared sitting in the armchair in my hotel room. I had not moved from my bed, but my consciousness was pulled out of my body and was kneeling at his feet by the side of the armchair in the corner of the room. He was a big and very strong man, with big features and large limbs. Stroking my hair, he said, "Not now. Now is not the time. You must wait three years." I bathed in his love for a moment longer and my consciousness was pulled back to my body.

My next encounter with Christ Maitreya was when someone handed me an article from a spiritual new age magazine. In it, an American woman had recounted her travel to London, England in a quest to find Christ Maitreya. In her article, she reported reading the story of someone who had visited with Christ Maitreya in a house in Marble Arch, a Middle-Eastern neighborhood in London. She shared the information with two of her friends, and together they decided to make a trip to London in pursuit of Christ Maitreya. Upon arrival at the airport, they took a taxi and asked to be taken to Marble Arch. When the driver asked exactly where in Marble Arch, they replied, "We will know it when we get there."

Once in Marble Arch, they chose an Indian restaurant to gather more information and to refresh themselves. Inside the restaurant, waiting to be served, each woman suddenly found their consciousness pulled out of their bodies. The sound of the voice of the waiter brought them back when he asked, "How can I serve you?" Returning to normal conscious state, each woman recounted their experience to one another. They each had left the consciousness of their bodies and found themselves kneeling at the feet of Christ Maitreya while he stood in a room alone with each of them. As they lifted their head from his feet, he placed his hand on their head and said, "I am here. You have found me. I will take care of you. Don't come looking for me, for you will not find me physically. Go back home and dissuade others from coming out in search of me. I can hear you and will answer you wherever you are."

The next thing they each remembered was the sound, the voice of the waiter in the restaurant, bringing them to their bodies. They sat around the table in the restaurant very quiet and absorbed in their thoughts for a while. Finally, they paid their bill, called another taxi, went to the airport and returned home to tell their tale.

That night after I returned home, I lay in bed praying and meditating. I remembered my last experience with Christ Maitreya and I said, "Master, I know you wouldn't want me to come to see you, but if you would give me permission, I would really like to know you and work with you. I long to be in your presence." Next, my consciousness was pulled out of my body. I was fully prostrated with my head on his feet. I could feel the warmth of his large and strong feet and the other-worldly fragrance that was permeating from his feet and his body. He placed his hand on my head, and I lifted my head and looked at his eyes. He raised his hand and pointed his finger at me, and very gently but firmly said, "Not now. Now is not the time. You must wait three more years." My consciousness was pulled back into my body in my bedroom and I realized that three years had gone by since my first experience with him.

While speaking with my friend Toni Maria one fall day in 2003, she told me that she had found a meditation group that gathered at a house ten minutes away from mine. Her father who now lives in the Midwest had highly recommended this meditation. I heard myself ask if I could join her. I was somewhat surprised at myself for asking because I am perfectly happy to meditate anywhere alone at any time. While driving with Toni Maria in her car on our way to the meditation group, I asked, "What kind of meditation is this?" She said, "Transmission meditation." When I asked, "What is transmission meditation and how is it different from other types of meditation?" she went into an elaborate account explaining that this was the meditation in which we receive the transmission from the Masters of Wisdom and the hierarchy led by the World Teacher, Christ Maitreya. "Christ Maitreya!" was the sigh that let out of my chest uncontrollably. Toni had now pulled her car into a driveway. No time to get over my shocked awe of what had transpired.

We were greeted at the door by a friendly couple and sat together around a table. We listened to the instructions given by our hosts, and a tape-recorded message. We were to recite the Prayer of the Great Invocation out loud together and sit in meditation for about one and a half hours to receive the transmission from the Masters of Wisdom led by the Christ Maitreya. The lights were dim, and I closed my eyes. Immediately my consciousness was drawn out of my body, focused on the figure of Christ Maitreya standing in front of me. Without further ado, he began a discourse relating to me, my life's mission, the books, publications, workshops, people to work with, places to go and things to do. He talked nonstop until the little angel bells announced the end of meditation.

Christ Maitreya has arrived and is here to stay. You will experience his presence through the chapters of this book. He makes his presence known. Masters are honored to invite and invoke his presence into circles, workshops, group and individual readings.

To feel his presence directly, sit in meditation and say The Great Invocation and allow the transmission to begin. Continue to say The Great Invocation daily to receive full benefits. If you wish, ask from the core of your heart that he will make his presence known to you in any way that he sees fit, and be patient. You will reap the harvest through patience and perseverance. Remember that he is the World Teacher, and as a teacher he is very gentle and loving, but he does take your personal will very seriously. If you are serious, you must ask and persist to receive his presence and his blessing.

I remember in one reading for two great members of one of my groups, Lord Metatron invited Christ Maitreya to bring a blessing to them. Christ Maitreya poured his energies into the room, and both recipients felt and received great love. Lord Metatron then relayed a message to them from Christ Maitreya that if they were willing to receive him daily in meditation, Christ Maitreya will awaken them between the hours of 4:00 and 6:00 in the morning and offer them his teachings and his energies for a while. This was a day in October on the east coast of the United States, right around the time when the cold weather sets in. After the session, the two participants looked at each other and conferred, "Oooh, getting up so early in the morning is not going to be fun," and, "Can we sit in bed and do it instead of getting up in the cold?" Right around then, I felt that the energy of that offer was withdrawn because there was resistance. I knew then that it would not happen.

I was on tour for a couple of months visiting New York and the east coast and leaving for Europe and India. When I returned, I had an email from one group member saying, " We were not woken up for our morning meditation after our reading. We take it that all is well since we were told that we need not do anything but we will be awakened by Christ Maitreya." Yes, that was absolutely true. You will be awakened when the time is right!

If you are ready and eager, the gifts will be bestowed upon you. If you have resistance, the gifts will be withdrawn, not as a sign of punishment, but as a token of love, in respect of your free will. When you are ready to offer that free will at the feet of the Masters and receive their blessings, you will do so with great joy, and they will bestow their gifts upon you. Remember then, if you are serious about walking on the path of light and desire to accelerate your spiritual growth, be consistent. Mean what you say and only say what you mean. Watch your personality and don't allow it to get in the way of the work of the Masters. Because even though your personality is the servant of your ego and the Masters know that, they will not interfere in the free will of your personality until and unless you choose to offer your free will up to God through the Masters and align your will with the divine will.

The most beneficial response in the above case would have been, "Your will be done." Failing that, "I would prefer to stay in bed and keep away from the cold in the early morning hours, nevertheless, not my will but thy will be done." This will give the Masters a chance to find the optimum beneficial solution to make you happy and serve the light.

Christ Maitreya has been waiting very patiently for humankind to receive him back on Earth. More than twenty years have gone by since the time that he has made himself available right here among us on Earth, and he is still patiently waiting. His offers to be interviewed by television and radio stations have been declined. His messages through his messengers have been disregarded. His miracles of the crosses of light and wells of miraculous healing waters are hushed. And his dignitaries sent to heads of states with proof of his existence have been ignored, as well as his requests to end war and world hunger. (For more information, read *Extraordinary Times, Extraordinary Beings* by Wayne S. Peterson.)

Christ Maitreya is still waiting. How long he waits depends on you and me. We have much work to do.

In The Presence of Christ Maitreya

Close your eyes for a moment and go deep within your own self. Feel yourself in the presence of the great assembly of the ascended masters and the energies of Christ Maitreya.

Now remember that you are merging and uniting with the essence of Christ Maitreya, the World Teacher. We offer all that we receive for the healing of Mother Earth and all humankind. We call upon the pillar of light, the ascended hosts of light, the cosmic beings of light and the cosmic light to hold us inside a bubble of pure white light. Only the highest and the purest of truth will be received and spoken through each one of us from this moment on.

Envision from the space of your heart chakra, the center in the middle of your chest, you are spinning the energies of the heart, spinning them and sending them upward. Envision from your solar plexus center (around the belly) golden light of the soul is spinning upward from within you. Envision from the area of your thymus gland, two to three inches below your throat, the energies of the cosmic heart where your spirit resides are spinning and spiraling upwards. And envision from the brain area the energies of the mind. These are all spiraling: the mind, the heart, the cosmic heart, the spirit and the soul are spinning outward and upward. You are inside the essence and the being of Christ Maitreya.

Christ Maitreya is that essence which ultimately we will all hold as our Higher Self. It is a consciousness that brings the recognition that you can attain mastery, and we are all united in oneness with God. As we spiral upward in the cylinder of light, we come before The Presence of The I AM THAT I AM. I AM THAT I AM is the presence of God in form. When you release all karma and are free from it you will step into levels of Mastery and merge into oneness in the essence of the I AM THAT I AM. Enlightenment comes after full Mastery is achieved. When you attain full enlightenment, you will live in total oneness with that presence at all times. That is when God Unity is achieved. Become aware of The Presence of The I AM THAT I AM and know that you have been brought to this point through the grace and intercession of Christ Maitreya.

Be still in this position and take a deep breath. Allow the energies to fill your body and your being. Sit in meditation for as long as you can and energize yourself with the heightened energies.

In your own mind become aware that the transmission is taking place by the ascended masters and mistresses of light, headed by Christ Maitreya. And we ask that the healing that is being administered to every member of this group and every member who has ever belonged to this group, or any other group that we have individually been involved with will also benefit from it. We would extend it further and say anyone that we have ever met and touched in any way, and everyone that we will continue to meet and touch can and will benefit from these high level energies if their Higher Self would allow it, if their I Am Presence would consider it right for them. Mention your loved ones, and ask for physical, mental, emotional and spiritual health in the body, mind, emotions, and spirit for yourself, your loved ones and for the group. All that we've done in service to light. So think of people, and put them in this triangle of light. Don't worry if you have 60 people creating a triangle. Our intention is to create triangles of light. We leave it in the hands of the masters exactly what the formation of the triangle might be.

Take a deep breath. Just feel the difference in the energy charge that is coming through. The texture of the energies has a different feel to it. It is very Christ-like. It feels the same way that it does when we go to the presence of the Brotherhoods and the Sisterhoods of the White Lodge.

Take a deep breath. Envision the presence of Christ Maitreya standing face to face with you. Take a deep breath and pause to still your mind and focus your heart in receiving Christ Maitreya.

And if it feels right in your heart, envision that you step into his presence as though you're going to walk into his body.

Enter into the etheric body and essence of Christ Maitreya. Pause for a moment and bathe in the Christ energies.

Say a prayer, ask for a gift, offer yourself in service to him and to the Masters of Wisdom. Offer your service to the light of the I Am through his intercession. Become still and feel the energies, and ask for a sign, a symbol, a word, a thought.

Be patient. If you don't receive a symbol the first time ask again, and pray with a sincere heart and an open mind that you can feel his presence and that he will show you the way to serve the light.

When you feel you are complete, thank The Presence of The I AM THAT I AM. Bless the presence of Christ Maitreya and ask that he will guide you and protect you from this moment on and through the rest of this life in the name of the I AM THAT I AM.

Take a deep breath and return to normal consciousness by feeling your energy return to your body. Shake your hands and your feet. Move about and enjoy the journey of discovery which awaits you through the pages of this book.

In The Presence of The I AM THAT I AM we invoke the highest aspect of Metatron which each one of us can hold and receive to come through into our bodies, so each one of us can receive the highest vibration of Metatronic light. The heart, the mind, the spirit, the soul, the cosmicheart are spiraling upward and outward from our merging with the energies of Christ Maitreya.

41

Divine Mother

Introduction

Divine Mother is an energy. It is the energy of the female force or the feminine principle of existence. It is this principle that takes form in the embodiment of the female to become impregnated with the creative force, the mother force.

When the breath of the divine spark is blown into the body of the feminine, the result is a Divine Mother who gives life to Divine Children and brings divinity into the world of form. In every age the principle of the Divine Mother takes form to bless the Earth with her presence and to anchor her creative energies of the feminine principle. Mother Mary, Mother Meera, Ammachi, Karunamayi and Quan Yin are all embodiments of that form.

In the book *Mother Meera Answers Part I*, Mother Meera speaks of the Divine Mother in this way:
"The Divine Mother answers our prayers. She has pure love for humans and protects them and promotes harmony and peace. When humans sincerely aspire for happiness, harmony, peace and light, then it is the Divine Mother who helps. She gives help for physical, mental, vital and spiritual well-being, giving peace, and helping people to obtain their needs. When humans on Earth are afflicted with difficulties, it is the Divine Mother who relieves suffering and lifts them up. The Earth always needs the Divine Mother's light and protection. She is a child that needs Mother's divine help." (p.20-22)

When asked, "Are there incarnations of the Divine Mother on Earth at this time?" she answers,

" Yes, many. Some will be known, others wish to remain secret. The work of each is different. Each expresses a different aspect of the Divine Mother. My scope is very broad and more integral. I help people at all stages of life and I also work with Sri Aurobindu and Sweet Mother. "

When asked, "What is the difference between the Divine Mother and the Divine Father?" she says,

"The Father is stricter, the Mother is more loving and soft. She is more patient than the Father and more accepting."

In the book *Memories of Beloved Mary-Mother of Jesus* by Thomas Printz, a collection of essays are gathered from the channelings of Geraldine Innocenti. In one essay, Archangel Gabriel says,

"I hold you within the compass of my arms and bring you the love of the Father as well as the love of the Divine Mother from whose bosom you came forth into individualization. You came with but one desire in your sweet, earnest hearts-to do their will, to carry the light and to be the full manifestation of their love."

In another passage, Gabriel says of Mother Mary,

"She developed a tremendous devotion to beloved Vesta. (Spiritual complement of beloved Helios, the one in charge of our physical sun. Beloved Vesta is the cosmic god-mother of our planet and of our system.) Mary virtually cradled the world in those

infant arms through the feeling of that Divine Mother-love, which she drew from beloved Vesta herself by her contemplation and love of that great being."

I sat to meditate with the Divine Mother energies one day in October of 2001 shortly after the disaster of September 11th. I had cancelled all my overseas commitments and travel arrangements. The prevalent energies were difficult to work with. People had become numb as a result of events, especially in the areas of the East Coast of the United States. New York, New Jersey and Massachusetts were my sphere of influence and where I lived at the time. Grave emotions mixed with panic and anxiety floated in the air.

I asked the Divine Mother for help to bring solace to all who were affected and help me with financial commitments while penalties for trip cancellations had left me with immediate need for reproach. She appeared to me in the way she always does, as a beautiful gentle loving Goddess figure inside tongues of fire. She said, "In three days, I will bring you resolution." By the third day nothing noticeable had happened so far as I could tell. The only event was a phone message with a request to teach two people levels two and three of a workshop immediately, because the originator of that workshop was coming to town the following month and was teaching the level four of that series. The requirements were completion of the first three levels, and I was qualified to teach those levels.

I had returned that message with another, informing the caller that I no longer taught that course and gave the name of someone who did. In the evening I sat down to meditate with the Divine Mother and said to her, "Mother, I have waited the three days and nothing has happened." She told me, "I brought you your solution and you refused it." When I inquired, she responded that she had sent me the people for the workshop. I protested by saying, "But I don't like teaching that class to two people only! The last time I taught it there were 34 people in the class. It takes a lot out of me to teach two four-day workshops to two people only. " Her reply was, "Well, if you do accept to teach it, I will bring a third person." I told her that I would do as she wished. However, I had already redirected them elsewhere. She said, "Do not worry. They will be back with the third."

The next morning I received a call informing me that now there was a third person and their preference would be for me to teach the course. When we went back and forth with available dates everyone was available immediately, willing to reschedule other appointments to make this happen. I received payments within the following two days and we started the course together.

The energies were intense and powerful. It was a very beautiful experience which ended with great love and friendships as well as a new business relationship that extended over the next three years. In the course of the days of the work, I didn't get the chance to follow up on the cancellation of the reservations, the related penalties and financial commitments. I was so charged by the energies that I had put aside my money worries while teaching the workshop. My mind was at ease that I now had the resources to pay for the penalties as the proceeds from the workshop came to the exact amount needed.

Divine Mother appeared to me while I was resting after the second workshop and said, "This was and continues to be an exercise in surrender. I would like you to trust that I will resolve your money dispute and instead, I would like you to use the money to build a rose garden on two patches of land in the yard." One was to be in the back yard in a circular shape dedicated to Mother Mary and in remembrance of the Divine Mother, and another one in the front yard in a square shape dedicated to the Lord Buddha in remembrance of Divine Mother and to balance the male and female energies. In the Buddha patch, I was to plant eleven deep dark red rose bushes and place in each corner one large piece of rose quartz weighing 20 pounds or more, with a statue of Lord Buddha in meditation pose in the middle. In the Mother Mary circle I was to plant 33 rose bushes all in light pinks and pastel colors and five pieces of rose quarts of equal weight and energy, with a standing statue of Mother Mary on top of a mound in the circle.

The most difficult task was removing the grass and digging the garden to prepare each patch, especially the circular mound. The most expensive part of the project was the purchase of the rose quartz pieces. I was almost out of breath and out of pocket by the time I had done those two. Since this was October, a very large tree nursery had a sale on their rose bushes. I could purchase 44 rose bushes at two dollars each. The problem was these were rose bushes which had seen the best of summer and had no more flower buds on them. Furthermore, the identifying tags relating the kind and color of the roses were missing.

I came back to the Divine Mother and told her that with $88.00 I could rescue 44 rose bushes from extinction, but I had no way of knowing which was what color. She told me, "Buy them all and bring them home. The rose bushes will tell you where they belong. Trust and surrender." I purchased 52 rose bushes which was the remaining supply in the nursery. It came to yet another auspicious number when I paid for them. (11, 33, 44, 88 and 104 are all very auspicious numbers.)

I made the circle and the mound and placed the statue of Mother Mary in the middle on top of a piece of gorgeous feldspar granite, which a friend gave me for the garden, and placed the five pieces of rose quartz around the base of Mother's statue. I said many prayers and began the work of sorting the plants out. The plants were all very responsive, and I had no difficulty sorting them out. I would ask them, "What color are you?" and they would give me an answer, and accordingly I would move them to the Mother Mary Circle garden or to the Lord Buddha Square Garden. I was doing this for a while when it began to get dark, and a light rain began to come down. To proceed faster, I started asking the plants, "Front or back?" and they would give me the answer.

I now had a good portion of them sorted out. A few were neither red nor pastel. These were the extras, and I was yet to figure out where they would go. Finally, the last rose bush told me it belonged to the front. I carried her to Lord Buddha patch and returned to the circle when I heard the voice from the Mother Mary statue tell me, "Go back and get that last one. It is not red. And bring her back here." I went dutifully and picked up the rose bush to bring it back when it said, "No. Put me down. I belong here." I put the plant down and went back to Mother Mary and said,

"Mother, she says she belongs to the front." Mother said, "She says that because she wants to be in the front yard, not because she is red. Go and bring her back here."

I stood there puzzled and said, "Well Mother, whatever happened to free will? Should I not give the plant her right of free will and let her stay in the front?" She replied, "No. In this case, the divine will supercedes the free will. That plant is not standing in the Truth. Go bring her back here." I brought her back and made a point of putting a marker next to her to distinguish her from the others since I now had to wait until next spring to bear witness to this saga. When I counted the numbers I had exactly eleven rose bushes in the front and 33 in back. Eight had declared they were yellow and bright orange, and these were going into a different bed. They went to a crescent-shaped patch around the front of a lilac tree to balance the patch in the opposite direction. Had I listened to the renegade rose bush, all the numbers would have been wrong.

The previous spring, I had made an angel garden according to the instructions from Master Jesus who wanted a small garden dedicated to the Seven Angels of Heavenly Father and the Seven Angels of Earthly Mother. I had a total of fourteen bushes planted around a lovely old pear tree and had called the fourteen angels to bless each plant.

The next spring was a time of surprises, all good ones. All the roses in Lord Buddha's patch were deep red, Mother Mary's were light pink and off-white, and the crescent patch roses were deep yellow and orange. The renegade bush came up with profusion of light pink flowers. I not only learned a lesson in trust and surrender, I also learned that even plants can disobey the Divine Will and cause havoc with choosing their own destiny. This is a lesson which they must have learned from their elders in the consciousness ring — "us", the human beings. I also learned that Divine Mother and Mother Mary can intercede on their behalf just as well as they do in ours!

Incidentally, roses are considered the highest of spiritually evolved species of flowering plants on Earth, after the lotus which is considered a divine messenger from the heavenly realms and the symbol for spiritual enlightenment. Such is the compassion of the Divine Mother. May your journey of rediscovery in the arms of the Divine Mother be showered with light and love from her heart.

Energies of Divine Mother Pouring Down to Earth

Commentary: This was part of a reading given to a young seeker traveling in India, about to visit the ashram (retreat) of Karunamayi, a living saint (avatar) and well-respected teacher (www.karunamayi.org).

METATRON, CHANNELED NOVEMBER 11, 2004

Beloved of my own heart, I am Metatron. Take a deep breath with me.

In the ashram of Karunamayi, you will come to touch the energy essence of the Divine Mother. It is very important that you open yourself fully to receive the energy of the Divine Mother. The Divine Mother essence is the creative force of this universe. The time has come for you to make yourself fully open to serving the energies of the Divine Mother. See her as the embodiment of all truth. See the physical embodiment of Karunamayi as the embodiment of the Divine Mother. Ask her to fill your heart with the knowing and the trusting that you are on the right path. Ask her to fill your heart with the energies of needlessness — needless of all human emotions, needless of all human desires, needless of all human wants, needless of all worldly treasures. Say this over and over again.

It doesn't mean you won't use these resources. It doesn't mean you won't live in this worldly realm. What it means is you would live in this worldly realm but not be of it. You will be in this world and not of it. This means that the resources of this world will not entice you. And the lack of those resources will not make you needy. When you come to that understanding, you would then have already come a long way in attaining that.

So my wish for you, in the name of the I AM THAT I AM, through the grace of the energies of Metatron and Ascended Masters of Light and Masters of Wisdom, is that you will find that elevated place of needlessness in humility and in total empowerment. That the power of divine grace showers every aspect of your being, that you may never be needy of human things, of human desires, of human urges, wishes, wants, and that no human, no place, no thing will distract you from your path, not even parents or children, friends or lovers. Not for a moment may you be delayed or distracted from walking the path of light and from serving the highest purpose on this pathway.

I promise you that I will be by your side. I will be walking ahead of you to clear the path for you. I will be walking behind you to make sure that you won't fall backwards. I will be holding your hand in my hand, to make sure that you know that you are provided for and that you are protected. And I open myself to you so that you can open your heart in trusting me. And in your trust, I will guide you.

Balancing the Male and Female Polarities

METATRON, CHANNELED AUGUST 18, 2003

Beloveds of my own heart, I am Metatron. Take a deep breath with me.

I bless you on this auspicious eve. The 18th of each month is an important landmark. On the day of the 18th in each month a shower of energies enters into the atmosphere of your planet. These showers of energy on the 18th of the month will continue to bring you higher vibrations of light. Mark your calendars and set aside time specifically on the 18th of each month to sit in meditation, saying the Great Invocation in the company of others or alone in agreement with others to do the same. At this present moment in Earth's history the 18th of each month is as important as the Full Moon and New Moon.

As you have been imbued by the masculine presence of the energies of Maitreya, I wish to present to you the Feminine Principal of Existence in the form of the energies of the Divine Mother. As I bring forth the energies of the Divine Mother, some of you may see her in form, others may just sense her presence or see a silhouette of light. On many occasions she presents herself inside flames of fire. On others she presents herself inside a body of water. This she does to bless whichever of the elements she chooses to present to you. This is her offering.

Together, we anchor the energies of the Divine Mother. Breathe deeply from the core of your being and allow me to present to you the energies of the Divine Mother, The Feminine Principle of Existence, The Creative Force of the Universe.

As you feel the presence of the blessed Mother in front of you, ask her permission and step forth and enter into the vibrational force field of the Feminine Principle of Existence. Bathe in the energies of light and ask for a balancing of your own male and female energies.

In the age where the Divine Mother presents herself in the form of Goddess Kali (Kali Yuga), humankind removes itself furthest away from its own divine origin. Many thousands of years of forgetfulness of your divine origin have brought you here. The energy of the planet has tilted in favor of masculine force. The physical, emotional, mental and spiritual bodies of all the souls that reside on the planet have become (energetically) masculine.

To return to your original blueprint, to remember as well as re-embody your divinity, you must return to a balanced point of equalities in the polarities of male and female. For this reason, request that the Divine Mother would balance your polarity fields in both male and female aspects.

If you wish to request this balancing for any member of your spiritual or blood-related family members, you may do so by calling upon their Higher Self. You may also request this healing on behalf of Mother Earth and all souls conscious and unconscious, sentient and insentient. And all the kingdoms planet-wide — kingdoms of minerals, animals and plants, kingdoms of simple organisms and complex ones, kingdoms of conscious and unconscious beings. Let us ask for a shower of light from the heartcore of the Feminine Principle. Remember to ask for yourself and on behalf of others. Ask for your future, path of service, comfort, prosperity, light, open heart, whatever individual wishes, desires and requests you can think of. Take a deep breath and express your wishes and meditate. Ask for a boon. Ask Divine Mother to give you a gift of her choice which will benefit you the most.

Elohim of Peace

Introduction

The Elohim are the architects and builders of our solar system. Known as "Angels of Divine Presence", the Elohim were called to bring the design and idea for our solar system into reality.

There are seven pairs of male and female Eloha (singular form) who make the Seven Mighty Elohim (plural). They are generally spoken of in plural form even when one is addressed. This is because each one is the equivalent of a great collective consciousness. The word Elohim is therefore the most popular way to address them. These are great cosmic beings whose power and might is beyond our imagination. They brought our solar system into form with great focus and cosmic determination. In cooperative effort among the seven pairs, they brought forth the divine manifestation of God's original idea envisioned by Helios and Vesta, the deities of our sun and the father/mother aspect for our solar system.

This book brings messages from Goddess Minerva, the Elohim of Illumination. Minerva and Cassiopia, her male counterpart arc the Elohim of the second ray, the Ray of the Wisdom of God. Lord Metatron invites the blessing of the Mighty Elohim of Peace in this book. Tranquility (male) and Pacifica (female) are the Elohim of the sixth ray, the Ray of Peace. Their contribution to the creation of our solar system is to bring forth the qualities and energy vibration of peace. In the first *Gifts* book, *Gifts from the Ascended*

Beings of Light, Lord Hercules, the Elohim of the first ray, gave his teaching and words of wisdom. Lord Hercules and Lady Amazon together create the quality of will to do and bring to Earth the energies of the will of God. The will of God is the first ray of manifestation among the seven rays with which this Earth and the solar system was built.

As you read the pages of these books and you come across these amazing cosmic beings of light, feel their love for this entire creation and ask them for guidance and assistance in your life. I make a habit of starting every invocation by saying, "In the name of the I AM THAT I AM, through the intercession of the Seven Mighty Elohim," and then I state whatever is relevant to the situation, or I go directly to my request. For example, my favorite one is to say, "In the name of the I AM THAT I AM, through the Seven Mighty Elohim, I call forth the Ascended Masters' attention to the issue of selling this house." "In the name of the I AM THAT I AM, I call for the intercession of the Seven Mighty Elohim to rectify the conflict regarding the family unit." Or in specific cases, I say, "In the name of the I AM THAT I AM, I ask the Elohim of Peace for a peaceful and easy day today. " Or, "In the name of the I AM THAT I AM, I call forth the Elohim of Illumination to bring light to today's meeting."

A great book on the Elohim is Thomas Printz's *The Seven Mighty Elohim Speak on the Seven Steps to Precipitation*. This is a book channeled by Geraldine Innocenti where the Elohim speak of the process of creating this solar system and teach how to manifest the object of your desires. The Elohim offer the same principles and ideas they used for creation and manifestation of this solar system to teach us how to materialize (precipitate) designs, ideas and thoughtforms in our reality.

Elohim of Peace

METATRON, CHANNELED AUGUST 18, 2003

Beloved of my own heart, I am Metatron. Take a deep breath with me.

In the presence of the Divine Mother, I now bring to your attention the energies of the Elohim of Peace and the consort, the feminine aspect, Pacifica. Envision standing in front of you two beings of light; one is the male and the other is the female aspect of The Elohim of Peace.. Envision that the two of them merge into oneness, and you see an angelic silhouette of a being made of pure white light.

With blessings from the Divine Mother, now step into this presence and ask that peace and harmony begin to vibrate at every cell, every molecule, every electron and every iota of your being and in all your body systems. Bathe in this light and let us together make the intention that the process of coming to peace will continue for as long as necessary. Let us also make the intention that in times of disharmony and conflict that the Elohim of Peace in male and female aspects make themselves available to us for a blessing that we may never lose the peace within our hearts and our minds. Different colored lights begin flashing, offering a shower of cleansing to all parts of your body. Pause and take a deep breath. Receive the energies. Ask for the gift of heal-ing. Ask for the gift of restoration to wholeness.

Notice as this blessing is received that there is another being of light directly opposite the energy field of the Elohim of Peace, and as we bow down together in thanksgiving and we turn around, you are now facing the energy field of the Elohim of Purity. The Elohim of Purity, Clair is the male aspect, and Astrea is the female aspect. Again, these two beings will merge and unite in oneness. As you stand facing them, take one step into their beingness and let us together make the intention for the purification of body, mind, emotions, heart, spirit and soul. Pause and take a deep breath. Feel the purifying energies move through you.

Ask for a boon, for a gift. Ask for purity of mind and spirit, body and soul, heart and emotions. Ask that all the scars of the past, present and future be released. Ask for the return to the purity and innocence that was intended by God in the original blueprint for the divine Hu-Man, God man and woman. Ask for the return of that purity. It matters not if in your process of purity others think of you as different, simple, naïve, too forgiving. Rather you were too forgiving than not. And let us together ask that the process of healing will continue for as long as necessary.

If you go back and stand in the center of this triangle where Mother the Divine is at one point and the Elohim of Peace and Purity are the other two points, turn clockwise from facing the Divine Mother to facing the Elohim of Peace to facing the Elohim of Purity facing back to the Divine Mother, bowing down and acknowledging their presence. Walk straight to the presence of the Divine Mother and step into her presence. Join and merge, unite in oneness, receive from the Eternal Mother the creative force of this entire universe. Pause and sit still for a few moments to absorb the energies from the Divine Mother.

As we begin the journey returning back into the pillar of light, in the presence of the "I AM THAT I AM," through the essence of Metatron, from the essence of the Metatron to the essence of the ascended hosts and Christ Maitreya, bathe once again in the energies of Christ Maitreya. Know that the transmission will continue for as long as necessary, to bathe you in your own mastery in light, as light, with light. And as you complete the journey of returning into your body, consider yourself the perfected essence of the human being, the divine being that God intended in the original blueprint.

In the days to come, remember that zinc will provide a layer of protection around your bodies and become a shield. Administer zinc to your diet. Remember the 18th of the month as the most important day of the month for transmissions of energies of higher vibration. Remember the Full Moon and the New Moon as the times of acceleration for the energies anchored in Truth. You may already remember the sleepless nights a day or two before, a day or two after each Full Moon and New Moon.

As the truth comes to the surface, all untruths have to be released and removed; therefore they too come to the surface. Remember that the energies of the new vibration for the golden age are being anchored as we speak. Remember that the events of the next few years in your individual lives depend upon what you choose to focus upon immediately in the days to come. You build your future with your thoughts, in each present moment. Think positive thoughts, plan joyful plans, fill your mind and your heart with light, call upon the ascended beings, masters, mistresses, the cosmic beings and the cosmic light itself. Remember to call upon the Cosmic Christ Fiery Heart Flame. Remember that the Cosmic Christ is active in this present point in the evolution of Earth.

May the light shine upon your path, may the blessing of the Divine Mother guide you, embrace you and bless you. In the presence of the assemblies of the ascended beings of light, the cosmic beings of light and the cosmic light, in the presence of Christ Maitreya, Elohim of Peace, Elohim of Purity, I stand with my arms spread holding you, blessing you, protecting you and loving you.

I am Metatron. So it is.

Melchizedek

Introduction

Known as the healer of the old by the scriptures, Melchizedek is our universal Logos, or the word for our universe. *In the beginning was the Word and the Word was with God, and the Word was God. (John 1:1)* He holds the highest place in the hierarchy of light beings after the presence of the I AM THAT I AM and Metatron. The I AM THAT I AM is the presence of God in form. Metatron, the great cosmic being of light, created this entire universe, and beyond, for the I AM THAT I AM to take form in.

This universe has many billions of galaxies. The Milky Way Galaxy, which has billions of star systems including our own solar system, is a very small galaxy inside this universe, and Melchizedek is its guardian. Dr. Karim Zargar in *Desert of Alchemy* states that in the Phoenician scrolls Melchizedek's name was Sydik. Melchizedek means "God is my king". He is known to be the father to the Seven Mighty Elohim, who are the architects of our entire universe.

In the books *Angels A to Z* by James R. Lewis and Evelyn Dorothy Oliver, he is called
"the celestial virtue of great grace whose function in Heaven is like the one Christ has on Earth." (p. 268)
According to the above, Melchizedek represents the holy spirit in the occult teachings. He is the prince of peace according to the Book of Mormon, and his symbols are a loaf of bread and the chalice. In the Gnostic *Book of the Great Logos* he is called Zorokothera, and in the Torah and the Bible

he is mentioned as the king of righteousness and the king of Salem (ancient name for Jerusalem). (ibid p. 268)

Believed to be a power greater than Christ, he came in human embodiment three thousand years before Christ to pave the path for the coming of Christ to Earth. He created education centers and mystery schools where the successful seekers would receive his teachings for a ninety-four year period in order to attain enlightenment. Seekers would learn to communicate with an enormous cosmic power called Melch. This enormous power was able to bring light to the core of darkness and release the dark eras from Earth, preparing the grounds for the appearance of Christ Light and Higher Consciousness. You may refer to either of my previous *Gifts* books where I have provided more extensive descriptions of Melchizedek.

Protection and Guidance Through the Sphere of Illumination

Commentary: This discourse was given to a high level initiate of the spiritual path and a very successful and disciplined businessman in the healing arts from New York. It is for those of you who wish to enter into the arena of service to larger audiences and expand your horizons. The focus of this discourse is to assist you to reach out in service to multitudes and masses. In this meditation, Christ Maitreya will bless your personal and global intentions for the future. Lord Melchizedek offers us several variations of this meditation for our specific needs.

MELCHIZEDEK, CHANNELED SEPTEMBER 11, 2004

Beloveds, I am Melchizedek. Take a deep breath with me.

61

Focus your awareness in the center of your heart. Envision an energy, a bubble, a sphere of deep, nile blue color, sitting in front of your heart chakra. The size of it is a small grapefruit. Inside of this luminous sphere is a white flame, much like a candle flame. At the very center it emanates golden beams of light throughout the sphere. I would like to ask your permission to etherically place this sphere in the center of your heart. The purpose for this exercise is:

1. To protect you in these days where you are in the business of giving of your life force and of your energy field and of your light;

2. To receive the illuminations and to know the guidance, because this sphere of illumination works at structural DNA level. It will decode your DNA to bring you the tools that you will need.

This is why ideas will come to you that you will put into practice, and they will be successful. Ideas that will help you take what you do to the next level and allow them to reach a much larger audience. If you wish to receive this sphere to protect you and to receive illumination at DNA structure of the body, say,

" Yes, I give permission."

We are now at the point where we need to reach critical mass. And in order to do that, it is important for you to set up your own individual grid and your own individual intention. And you are a master at that. The procedure is to work and design an idea into a series of thoughtforms which can then be brought into this reality by setting your focus on it, by moving your energies through it, by embodying its ideal design. And bringing that embodiment into this physical reality — moving it from thoughtform to the realm of action. It is important for you to visualize that. It is important for you to accept, if you will, this next phase of spiritual growth on behalf of the planet, on behalf of all those that you touch, and on behalf of your own soul. Your soul is yearning now to move to that next level, and this is why sometimes you feel as though you need to do something beyond what you have done so far. And yet there is a part of you that would rather be calm and enjoy life and reap the harvest of your many years of efforts.

However, those of you who are at levels of Mastery are not here to stay and be calm. You are always in action. You have to be in action because your actions are needed. You have to be in action because your focus and your intent is on the light and the life force, because your intention is pure, because your ultimate goal is to bring union — the light of God, the light of realizing the self, the light of Mastery. And because of that, beings such as yourself are in great demand right now, and unfortunately you won't have time to take a respite. You will always be pleased in your own heart for what you have gained and what you have achieved and what you have given.

By receiving this sphere of illumination and by allowing it to decode inside of your body, you will begin to see that design and the idea extend and expand from the level that you have established right now. The design which is already anchored on the earth plane, to the next level of anchoring where you would allow larger audiences to receive from you. It will mean changes and shifts in a lot of ways. But it will all be beneficial. The time has now come for you to reach to multitudes and masses. Knowing the complete purpose of the sphere, would you allow me to activate it now? If you wish to receive this activation, say, " Yes. "

Focus in the center of your heart. An energy, a bubble, a sphere. Colors: blue-deep, nile blue. Sitting in front of your heart chakra. The size of it is a small grapefruit. Inside of this luminous sphere is a white flame, much like a candle flame. At the very center it emanates golden beams of light throughout the sphere. Take a deep breath. Envision this sphere of blue light. You might be feeling that your body is becoming lighter. You might be feeling a sensation run through your bodies.

I am going to begin to spin this sphere. Imagine an imaginary axis that goes north-south, a thread of light that holds the center of this sphere together, and that's where that flame resides. And this sphere will spin from the left of your body to the front of your body, to the right, to the back of your body — that is the rotation of the spin. It is not quite clockwise, but it is in that type of a spin around the central axis. And as it begins to spin faster and faster it creates an energy, a vacuum around it where it will interact with your heart and your heart chakra. And at some point, as the spin comes to its full velocity, you'll find that this sphere is vacuumed into the heart chakra. And at that point, there is an explosion of pure white light. Breathe that explosion and know that at that point the sphere has become part of your being. It is no longer an external object.

And when the explosion happens, there's a ripple effect that sends out waves, like a pebble that has been thrown into the center of the ocean. And it is sending out waves of energy and movement, rippling outside. And there's a pulse. It is a wave-pulse pattern. You feel the wave in your body. You feel the pulse in rhythm with your heartbeat. Sit with this for a moment. Feel it and scan your body from top to bottom and feel how it is impacting every cell of your body. Pause and take a deep breath and feel the wave and pulse move through your body and beingness.

And with your permission, as you are beating your heartbeat with the pulse of this Sphere of Illumination, I would like to call upon the presence of Christ Maitreya, energies of Christ Maitreya, energies of Maitreya Buddha to come and join us. I would like to ask you to feel the presence. And again, the presence of Maitreya will interact and intermingle with the sphere of illumination in your heart. And I ask that you open up at DNA level by commanding your own DNA to open up to receive the energies of Maitreya, the Christed self. In the presence of Maitreya, ask for your global and personal intentions. Pause and meditate, asking for your intentions.

Every morning upon awakening, bring your attention to the sphere of illumination and begin spinning this sphere. And begin moving energy from your power center in the solar plexus by taking a deep breath. One deep breath moves energy from the solar plexus to the personal heart. Inhale and exhale. One short breath lodges the energy in the center of the heart. One deep breath from the personal heart to the cosmic heart, the thymus gland. One short breath lodges it in the thymus. One deep breath moving the energy from the thymus to the throat. One short breath lodges it in. One deep breath from the throat to the third eye. One short breath lodges the energy in to the center of the ajna, the third eye. One deep breath takes the energy to the crown. Short breath holds it in the crown chakra.

From there, we move with one deep breath, visualizing the center heartcore of Mother Earth, connecting from left and right, top and bottom, front and back. Beams and threads of light from the heartcore of Mother Earth are moving out in every direction throughout the solar system. One deep breath takes it through to the central sun of your system. As you move to the central sun, become aware of the presence of the male and female deities for your sun, Lord Helios, Lady Vesta. Merge your energies into the presence of the logos, the word for your system, the male and female aspects. Pause for as long as you wish, as long as you would like to exchange energies, as long as you would like to invite Lord Helios and Lady Vesta to communicate with you. Some days this is how far you go. Some days you may take it to the next level.

Going now from the central sun of your own system to the central sun of the galaxy. One deep breath takes you to the galactic sun. Become aware of the presence of Lord Melchior, Lady Melchai, the male and female deities of the central sun for your entire galaxy. Again, some days you become aware of their presence, and they have something to tell you in exchange. And some days you'll just greet them and bless them and be blessed by them and move on.

One deep breath will take you to the central sun of the entire universe. Melchizedek and Lady Malak are the deities. You all have your own deep connections with Melchizedek. The surface of your vision is pouring with nile blue light. Some days you may pause here for a long time, and we will have an exchange together. Some days you may greet me and move on.

One deep breath will take you to the great central sun of this entire cosmos and the presence of Alpha and Omega.

It may be a while before Alpha and Omega will show their presence in any form tangible by the human mind. Luminous platinum colored light will come to the surface of your vision. Presence of Omega, the feminine aspect, is the ultimate creative force of the universe. Presence of Alpha is the ultimate masculine. The greatest focus, the laser-beam of focus, that which brings to physical manifestation is the energy of Alpha. And the energy of Omega is the pure light and the pure dark, all in one. Omega is the pure everything-ness, the pure is-ness.

At each of these stops or stations, you can put in your personal intention, your global intention, your universal, omniversal, cosmic intentions. Your 3-year plan, your 10-year plan, whatever you choose. Put in whatever comes to your mind.

Once you feel complete in this final phase, then become aware of your return journey. Onc deep breath brings you back from the center of the cosmos to the center of the universe. One short breath, pause and return. One dcep breath brings you from the center of the universe to the center of the galaxy. One short breath, pause and return. One deep breath brings you from the center of the galaxy to the center of the sun of your own solar system. One short breath finalizes. One deep breath brings you to the core of Mother Earth. One short breath anchors the energies from the cosmic, the universal, the galactic and the central sun levels into the heartcore of Mother Earth. One short breath will complete that phase. One deep breath, back to your crown chakra. Then coming down the chakras, take short breaths. At crown chakra take a short breath, and continue with short breaths to third eye, throat, cosmic heart and personal heart. At the central sun of your own body, your solar plexus, take a long breath. Final completion.

If you would do this every day, you'll see the acceleration take a whole new level. You'll see that your work and your growth and your own evolution take a whole new turn. At each of these stations, become aware of the presence of Christ Maitreya, Maitreya Buddha. Bring that presence with you from station to station, from moment to moment.

Manifesting With the Blue Sphere of Illumination

Commentary: This is a meditation given for when we have a specific plan or project in mind that we would like to manifest. We may call upon the presence of Christ Maitreya as well as the Great Silent Watcher to hold our plan or project until it comes to fruition.

MELCHIZEDEK, CHANNELED SEPTEMBER 12, 2004

Beloveds, I am your brother Melchizedek. Take a deep breath with me.

Envision in front of your heart chakra a ball of light the size of a small grapefruit. The color is bluish-purple, or Nile blue. In the center of this sphere there is a flame like a candle flame. That is the spark of God unity, the spark of the Christos, the Christed self, which illuminates in the center of this sphere. This sphere is the Sphere of Illumination. Its job is to bring you the decoding of your DNA structure to release the memories of your own masterful essence back into your bodies, to retrieve the conscious-ness of the Higher Self, the God Self, the Divine Self. This Sphere of Illumination will also help you in the release of all the karmic entanglements that have been created according to the Law of Cause and Effect. It will be the dissolution of all those webs that you have woven throughout eons of time; lifetimes from which you need to be released, to become the pure and innocent masters of light and to return to your Divine Self. You have free will to receive this sphere or not. Do I have your permission to reestablish the Sphere of Illumination in the heart of each one of you individually? If you would like to give permission, say, *"Yes."* Take a deep breath and prepare to receive the blue sphere.

Envision that this sphere is spinning around a north-south axis. Envision that a thread of light runs through the center of this sphere. The sphere is spinning around that thread. The sphere is positioned about five inches outside of your body, spinning, right in front of your heart chakra. It is moving from the left of your body to the front of your body, to the right of your body, to the back of your body. The spin is from left to right and around, and it is going to become faster and faster. As it becomes faster, the color moves from being dark blue to light blue to pure white.

At the point at which it reaches pure white, a vacuum force is created that pulls this sphere into your heart center. At that point you will feel the vibration of an explosion that moves into a wave pulse. An explosion in the heart center extends beams of light in all directions. Like a little pebble that you have thrown in the water, reaching from the top of your head to the tip of your toes, tips of your fingers; wave-pulse, wave-pulse. Like a little pebble that you have thrown in the ocean. The ripples wave outward from the center. The rhythm of the pulse beats in unison with your heartbeat. Become aware of your heartbeat. Feel the wave moving into your body. Pause and take a deep breath. Feel the wave pulse.

As this vibration moves, beaming out from your heart in all directions, it moves out of your body, into the energy of the room, from the room into the town, from the town into the globe, moving around Mother Earth, into the heartcore of Mother Earth. The wave is pulsing from the heartcore of Mother Earth, all the way moving around in the solar system. It pulses first to the planets on either side of Earth — Mars and Venus — then to the planets on either side of Mars and Venus, all the way moving around. Take a deep breath.

The wave pulse reaches into the heartcore of the sun of your solar system or what we call the central sun. Lord Helios and Lady Vesta are the deities of the sun. As you go straight into the heartcore of the sun blazing the light, find yourself in the Great Hall of the Great Temple, the Helios Temple. Being received by the presence of Lord Helios and Lady Vesta, receive your gift. Say your prayer. Ask for a boon. Pause for a moment and absorb the energies. Meditate in the presence of Lord Helios and Lady Vesta. Listen to their words. Feel their energy. Become aware of your own beingness and your own vibration of light in their presence.

If you have a plan or a project that your heart is set on, a desire or an idea that you have been thinking about, at this point ask that Lord Helios and Lady Vesta would intercede on your behalf. Give them this design, this project, this thought, this plan and ask for the presence of the Great

Silent Watcher. The Great Silent Watcher is a great being, whose job it is to hold the force of a thoughtform to bring that thoughtform into existence. When Lord Helios and Lady Vesta wanted to create this central system — your solar system — they brought their design and idea to the Great Silent Watcher. The Great Silent Watcher held that design within her own womb, within her own heart, within her own mind for eons of time, for that seed to become the reality you now know as your solar system. A being of this caliber can hold on to your design and your idea and bring it into manifestation. If you can trust, it will be done. Surrender that through the intercession of Helios and Vesta, the Silent Watcher would hold your design, your idea, your thoughtform, and bring it into manifestation. Offer it with all of your heart and mind. And know that it has already taken root, and if it is your highest wisdom it will manifest.

We offer a blessing and a prayer of thanksgiving to the presence of Helios and Vesta, the deities of our sun, and to the Great Silent Watcher, the great cosmic being who held the design for this entire solar system including your Mother Earth in her heart until it came to manifest from the ethers. In the future, if you ever have a program, a project, a plan, a design or idea that you so wish to manifest, remember that you can come to the presence of Helios and Vesta, ask their intercession, and call upon the Great Silent Watcher to hold that design within her own being until it comes into manifestation. As human beings we are fickle. We think of things and then we forget about them. As a great cosmic being, the great central sun and the Great Silent Watcher will not forget the design and idea that you would like to manifest. We bless them and we thank them.

So we take our leave. The energy is moving outside of the solar system into the central system of the galaxy. This time we simply bow down to the presence of Lord Melchior (Mel-ki-yor) and Lady Malkai (Mel-ka-ee) as we move through the central system of the galaxy into the central system of our universe and into the presence of Melchizedek, Lady Malak. At this level put in a universal intention. Pause. Take a deep breath and think of a universal prayer. May peace reign throughout the universe. May the light of the I AM THAT I AM spread throughout this entire universe, in the name of the I AM THAT I AM, through the intercession of the Seven Mighty Elohim and the attention of the Ascended Masters and Great Beings of light.

There is a lot of turmoil in this quadrant, which we call our universe. I ask of you to put in an intention for peace, universal peace. There is a lot of warring going on between the various factions of light and the various factions of dark. Your intentions to bring forth peace will be heard and acted upon by the hierarchies. **Peace is the divine right of every soul. You must will it to come about.** You must command it to reign in your lives, whether in your individual life, your country, your planet and even at the interplanetary, solar, galactic and universal levels.

Summary: Every day make a point of repeating this meditation. First, invoke the presence of Christ Maitreya; ask for a blessing. Then begin to spin the Sphere of Illumination, which is already illuminated and spinning in your heart. Begin by taking one deep breath, moving the energy up chakra by chakra, one deep breath takes you from the heart to the throat. One deep breath takes you to the third eye. One deep breath takes you to your crown. The energy of the sphere is decoding and expanding the pillar of light, extending itself outside of your body. One deep breath from the crown charka to reaching into the presence of your Higher Self. From your Higher Self, take one deep breath and move to the Presence of the I AM THAT I AM. In the Presence of the I AM THAT I AM, moving energies to the heartcore of Earth, blessing Mother Earth, extending and expanding in all directions. Moving through the ring that is your solar system, reaching with one deep breath to the sun in the presence of Lord Helios and Lady Vesta, pausing for as long as you wish. Moving with one deep breath to the presence of Melchior and Lady Melkai, the galactic core, one deep breath moving to Melchizedek and Malak the universal core, one deep breath moving to the cosmic level, Alpha and Omega. Bringing the Christed force in the presence of Lord Maitreya, offering a prayer, cosmic prayer. Returning back with one deep breath, bring your energies from cosmic to universal aspect. Then with one deep breath from universal to galactic, one deep breath from galactic to solar, one deep breath from solar to global, one deep breath from global to your physical body. One deep breath from your crown chakra descending; third eye, throat, thymus, heart chakra, send it even further down to bless the energies in the solar plexus, sacral plexus, the root chakra; move it back up and let it lodge in the thymus gland.

With this meditation, you will allow the decoding of your DNA structure. You connect with the Masters of Wisdom, bring in the transmission to the world, anchoring it on Earth. Touching with it everyone, everywhere and everything that comes your way in the course of the day. If you decide in your meditation in the morning to keep this connection open either at the solar level, the galactic level, at the universal level or at the cosmic level, leave it open. When you get back to it at night, start from your core being all the way to those levels, but bring it back and close it at the end of your meditation. Again, if your own instruction and guidance that you receive from the Masters is to leave it open, just bring the energy into your body, knowing that your connection with those levels is maintained. If you are told to close the loop, then go all the way up and bring all of the energy back and anchor it back into your body.

With great love, with great joy in the celebration of what we are together, in the celebration of the presence of the Masters of Wisdom, I am your brother, Melchizedek. So it is.

(Note: The Summary of Manifesting With the Blue Sphere of Illumination Meditation is a great summary given by Melchizedek. It covers all the steps for the meditation, and the breathing has been simplified in this version. You can use this summary for your daily exercises.)

Mantra to Bring Forth the Light of Truth Before the Presence of Christ Maitreya

MELCHIZEDEK, CHANNELED SEPTEMBER 11, 2004

Beloveds, I am Melchizedek. Take a deep breath with me.

Every day in the course of your day, become aware of the presence of Christ Maitreya and call forth the energies of truth and say over and over again,
"May the truth of light be known.
May the truth of God be known.

May the truth of God be spoken.
May the truth of Christed Maitreya Buddha
reign on Earth now and forever. "

Make this your mantra with every breath. The energies of truth must be anchored. All the untruth has to be released; hence, all the violence, all the abrasiveness, all the bloodshed.

It is a rule that has been accepted by the collective consciousness of humanity that blood cleanses. Let us override that rule by calling upon the light of truth to cleanse. May the truth cleanse the world of all sadness and sorrow, of all fear and pain, of all violence. May the light of truth shine in every heart. May the light of truth cleanse the minds, the hearts, the hands of all souls from all pain, from all sorrow, and from all fear.

In love, in celebration and in thanksgiving for all that you are and all that you do — most of which is unrecognized by this third-dimensional realm — we celebrate you with all of our hearts and all of our being. In moments of doubt, turn your face to us. In moments of fear, turn your face to us. In moments of weariness, turn your face to us. Call upon Christ Maitreya. Call upon Helios and Vesta. Call upon Melchior and Melchai. Call upon Melchizedek and Malak. Call upon Alpha and Omega. Call upon the Ray of Truth. Call upon your own Presence of the I AM THAT I AM, in the name that you are.

In the name and in the perfection of I AM THAT I AM, I stand with folded arms. I am your brother, Melchizedek. So it is.

Mother Mary

Introduction

Mother Mary is an Ascended Master and mother of Ascended Master Jesus. Held in reverence by the Christians in the western world, she is considered an aspect of Divine Mother. She is known to be the Queen of Heaven for all the work she performed in raising the light of the world and for her service to humankind. Evidence discovered through the Dead Sea Scrolls shows that Mother Mary was a great Essene (Ess-een) teacher and healer. The Essenes were a highly evolved spiritual group of people who lived in the area known as Qumran in present-day Israel.

Mother Mary's own mother Anna was also a teacher and healer of her own time, and she brought up her daughter Mary in the ways of the Essene. Purity of body, mind and emotions were of utmost importance in teachings of the Essene. The great plan of God for Mary and her offspring was known to her and her mother Anna, who was a seer. Anna knew of the principle of immaculate concept and planned to raise her daughter to be the embodiment of the immaculate concept and to carry it in her womb. The essence of the immaculate concept is the pure and original design as God intended for humanity according to the Divine Plan. This is the plan where humankind was made in the image of God and maintained the concept of virgin birth. Virgin in this instance applies to pure and innocent birth of God as human. The word human itself carries both

God and mankind's energies, i.e. Hu-man-kind. Hu is an ancient and sacred name of God, similar to El.

The Essene had a very deep spiritual faith and were in constant communion with the angelic forces and the Masters as well as the great Heavenly Father energies and the Earthly Mother energies. They knew that balance of male and female polarities was a necessary component of life and the path to liberation. They worshiped and revered both female and male aspects of God as Heavenly Father and Earthly Mother. Master Jesus was taught these principles by his Mother Mary who herself had learned them from her mother Anna. The *Essene Gospel of Peace* by Edmond-Bordeaux Szekely is a translation of the teachings of the Essene. Master Jesus recites the prayer of Our Father followed by the prayer of Our Mother. I have printed these in *Gifts II* and gone into greater details of the life of Mother Mary as a student of the Essene school and as a Master Teacher of the Essene ways in her later life. After the passing of Jesus, Mother Mary has been traced to travel in the Middle East, healing and teaching extensively. There is a small basilica in Ezmir, Turkey where it is believed that Mother Mary spent the last few years of her life. I have given an account of visiting this site on Mother's Day in the year 2000 in *Gifts II*.

In the following pages Mother Mary gives an account of the process of Ascension and the various stages of Mastery before Ascension is achieved. She explains that what New Age literature collectively calls Ascension should in fact be called Mastery. Before we can ascend we have to become Masters, and before we become Masters we have to become initiates and disciples of the Masters. There are indeed many levels of initiation which lead to Mastery and then Ascension. I have explained these in the Introduction. Mother Mary relates Mastery to the birth of a baby and the stages of growth to full adulthood. If Ascension could be likened to full adulthood, the present consciousness of the masses of humankind is a newborn baby (unawakened souls). Therefore to expect humanity to make its Ascension any time soon would be to expect a toddler to attend post graduate study courses. Mother Mary explains the Ascension of Earth as a planetary body in the following section.

On Ascension

Commentary: Someone asked Mother Mary to define Ascension and her response is what follows.

MOTHER MARY, CHANNELED AUGUST 26, 2004

My beloved children of light, I am Mother Mary.

To give you a description of the word Ascension, first I suggest that you find the dictionary meaning of that word. (Dictionary: To ascend is to move above, upward or to move beyond, i.e. ascend to the throne. Ascension is the process of moving above or beyond. In Christianity the bodily rising of Jesus into Heaven on the 40th day after his resurrection. A feast celebrating this event, observed on Ascension Day. Ascension-noun: the act of rising or moving upward.) Add to my description the vocabulary meaning, and you will understand why that word does not apply to the present state of the consciousness of humankind or the planet.

In a religious sense, there is a description of the feast of the Ascension of Mary that has been allotted to the month of August. When the soul on its final embodiment reaches a level beyond the karma — the need to incarnate into physical embodiment — and fulfilled its divine purpose, then it can ascend to higher realms of being. Let me address the processes for reaching Ascension.

Imagine a newborn child. First it has to hold its head upright, then it can roll over, then it can sit upright, then it can crawl, from crawling to standing up, then it takes its first step in walking. Then it will be able to walk a few steps holding its balance with difficulty, then with ease, then at stride all the way through various phases to adulthood. In the same way, for a new soul to achieve Ascension, it needs to go through all these phases of evolution. The majority of the souls that are on the planet are in their toddler phase from the perspective of spiritual growth.

Those who have awakened to the knowledge and the wisdom that God resides within your own heart and soul have graduated from the toddler phase to standing upright. Souls move from a teenager phase to their young adult phase when they shift to the wakefulness of devoting their lives to service. No longer amassing wealth in self-interest, they devote their lives to the needs of the masses after having provided for their own needs and the needs of their loved ones. Those who become the teachers and Masters of the spiritual path and begin to gather their followers and access higher realms as true spiritual Masters are equivalent to reaching middle age. They have reached Mastery. Those who complete many lifetimes of Mastery and no longer need to come in another incarnation reach Ascension. This is Ascension of a human soul.

To recap in simple formula, a human soul goes through the following phases to reach Ascension. First, a human soul awakens to the knowledge of good and bad, light and dark, and the knowledge that God resides within the self. To serve that God within the self, one needs to help others and treat others as oneself. A person becomes awakened at that phase. Before that phase there is the phase of sleepfulness. This is the phase where humanity does not have knowledge of the light within their own heart. Ninety-nine point nine percent of the population of Earth is still in that level of existence. They are surviving, not serving.

You will read in the Metatron chapter about the Masters' attempt to spiritually awaken one percent of the population of Earth by August 2005. This is why Christ Maitreya and Sanat Kumara are so intently active, guiding and directing the Masters of Wisdom to assist humanity to reach that one percent level. Metatron tells us that critical mass can then be achieved for all the souls. The domino effect of the critical mass will ignite the divine spark in the hearts of all souls. This is the greatest of good news for all of us who have been waiting for the evolution of the consciousness of the masses to higher light, and it sets us off into the thousand years of peace. Metatron has stated that the entry point to the thousand years of peace is Spring Equinox — March 20, 2005.

The purpose of this book is to help the fully awakened souls and initiates — such as yourself — to connect with the Masters, become their disciples, and lead the masses. Through the guidance of the Masters, you can help newly-awakened souls become initiates of the Masters and raise their consciousness. Refer to the message of April 3, 2004 in the Metatron chapter. When one moves from the sleep of ignorance and awakens to his/her divinity, it is only the first step in the direction of Ascension. After awakening, one faces the great battle with the duality of this world, i.e., recognition of good and bad, understanding of service as opposed to self service, sacrifice in interest of others as opposed to self-interest and devoting one's life to raising the consciousness of the multitudes and masses. At those levels one moves from simple wakefulness through different phases of Mastery.

There are many levels and hierarchies even in the process of Mastery. The Masters differ from one another with respect to their levels of Mastery, their viewpoint and their mission of service. This is when the God above becomes the God within. The Master becomes compassionate upon the recognition that the God within is shining through every individual soul, even if the soul is asleep. Recognizing the God in each individual soul and allowing the spark of God to shine even when someone does something out of ignorance; that is the job of a Master.

This is why living Masters such as Ammachi, Sai Baba, (avatars) and spiritual Masters and leaders such as Dalai Llama (the spiritual leader of Tibet) have devoted their entire life in giving their light to others, serving others, helping others, selflessly. When a soul attains the final levels of Mastery, it becomes filled with light. The soul, so filled with the light of God, can no longer be contained in physical embodiment. At that point, a soul in embodiment leaves the body and ascends.

The literature available in New Age circles speaks of attaining one's Ascension in embodiment. As a general rule that definition of Ascension really relates to the attainment of Mastery. One can attain Mastery and still remain in human embodiment. But when the amount of light or the quotient of light that shines through a human being reaches the level of 100%, that light could burn the body (in the present polluted environment of Earth). It no longer is necessary for a soul that vibrates the illumination of that much light — a hundred percent pure light — to maintain a body of matter, because at the level of 100% light you are no longer bound by matter. The laws of matter do not apply any more. A soul of that level can take a body of matter or drop it off at any given moment. There are, of course, highly evolved souls who take physical embodiments at will, after their Ascension to serve the masses and to bring final Ascension to Earth. These are exceptions to the rule.

An example is the highly evolved soul known as Saint Germain who delayed his Ascension by more than 300 years because of his wish to serve humanity and Mother Earth. He was involved with the building of the foundation for democracy and the arrival of souls who would incarnate in the land of the Americas to promote freedom. Why did he live in that body for 300 years? He made a selfless service and sacrifice on behalf of humanity and Earth. When he finally took his Ascension at the end of that lifetime, he remained very close to Earth and very specifically he keeps close watch upon the land of the Americas and all the souls that incarnate there. It was his choice and his project to raise the vibration of that land and to call to it souls that would serve the globe and help in the Ascension process of Mother Earth.

Ascension of Earth

Commentary: After discussing Ascension at the individual level for humankind, Mother Mary continued her discourse by applying the same concept to Mother Earth and the other planetary bodies.

MOTHER MARY, CHANNELED AUGUST 26, 2004

My beloved children of light, I am Mother Mary.

The Ascension process of Earth is, again, a term that is used out of its exact context. If Earth were to attain her Ascension, it would become pure white light. At that point it would no longer be this dense body of matter. Therefore it would no longer hold souls which come in dense bodies of matter. Ascension of Mother Earth retold in the new age literature is in actuality the Mother Earth moving from awakened state to her divine state. She is moving through the various phases of her evolution to surpass duality — the knowledge of good and evil — and to then embody divine love. At which point she, as the planet who is hosting all of you, will attain her full mastery. Once full mastery is attained, a planet can move through the phase of Ascension. The actual process of Ascension in linear terms may take a thousand years or more.

Master Jesus has related in the Bible the coming of the thousand years of peace. That signifies the progression to Ascension. The Earth is still in physical embodiment at that point. There is still the duality of good and bad, night and day, light and dark. With the peace, the good shall reign and the bad shall be imprisoned. The night shall fall but the day shall be in full bloom. The bad will be known but the good shall reign. This is why symbolically it has been said that when the thousand years of peace arrive, the evil will be trapped and imprisoned, put in a dungeon and the door to the evil and the knowledge of evil will be sealed for a thousand years.

When the new age literature speaks of Ascension of Earth, the term refers to Earth as a consciousness coming to terms with her own Mastery. As planetary bodies go, Mother Earth is going through her own rite of passage, attaining and achieving Mastery. Relating this to my example of growing from birth to a senior citizen, the Ascension of Earth refers to reaching full adulthood — the equivalent of a human 35 years of age who has had the experience of childbearing and childrearing.

What needs to be reflected upon more so than the definition of Ascension is the definition of Mastery. Because what you mean when you say, "The Earth will ascend," or "Ascension of human beings," really is when the Earth will attain her Mastery and human beings will attain their individual Mastery — the best result that you could hope for at this present moment on Earth. If true Ascension is to be achieved, ultimately everything will turn into pure white light. This physical body of matter in this shape or in any shape will no longer be of any importance, whether it is the physical body of a human being, a blade of grass or of the Planet Herself.

To summarize, in order to move into levels of Mastery, you first have to achieve awakening of the multitudes and masses. And in order to awaken the multitudes and masses, you need a minimum number of human beings, souls that are willing to devote their lives to the service of awakening all the other souls. There are many steps before you get to the top of the mountain, and every one of those steps is important in its own right. To get to the top of the mountain, you first have to take a footstep and leave your footprint at the bottom of the mountain while you are still standing in the valley.

The multitudes and the masses that live on Earth have not yet awakened to their knowledge of the Divine spark within their own hearts. The numbers of those who have awakened to this knowledge are small. Small enough that they cannot hold space for the entire population to be pulled into Mastery. However, the greater your focus and your desire to make this process happen and to reach the end result — Ascension — the greater the results.

I have given you a long explanation that may seem difficult to achieve. However, when you achieve the full awakening of the multitude and masses and raise the consciousness of the planet through each individual soul, it will be the greatest step. It is that most important first step in achieving Ascension. To have Ascension, you have to focus on this first step. And in order to achieve that first step, you all have to realize what an important sacrifice it is to devote your lives to service. To devote your life to service, you have to perform your mundane level tasks to perfection and to finish off your karma.

The Ascended Masters are your own brothers and sisters of light, who have fully attained Mastery and moved away from physical embodiment. Their souls have attained a hundred percent degree of light within the body of matter. These Masters are here to help you. With the help of the Ascended Masters who have moved away from being incarnate and of the Masters who are presently in physical embodiment, as well as their disciples — which are all of you — we will move this planet to wakefulness, raising consciousness to levels of Mastery to final Mastery, to full Ascension.

I love you all for your high horizons and your enormous hearts and your great desires to reach to that top step, to the top of the mount. I love you for your persistence and perseverance, and I love you for all the devotion that you give to your work. I ask you not to be disheartened by the number of steps from here at the bottom of the valley to the top of the mount. I remind you that this is a journey of discovery, and in the process you will have great adventure, great wisdom, great knowledge. Even when you have great pain, great suffering and great sorrow, it adds to your knowledge of life, appreciation of life and participation in life.

In love and light, in joy and in sorrow, in pain and in pleasure, I stand at your feet as your Mother Mary. And so it is. It is done. Amen.

Quan Yin

Introduction

Quan Yin is the Goddess of compassion and mercy. She has been an Ascended Master, and in the Orient she is loved and revered as a Divine Mother. Her pictures and statues have traditionally adorned altars in homes, shops and businesses everywhere in the East and more recently in the West as well. Quan Yin ascended from Earthly realms over 14,000 years ago. During those years Quan Yin devoted her life to the guardianship of the seventh ray, which is the most important ray active at this present juncture of Earth's evolution. For all that time her focus has been the anchoring of the seventh ray on Earth.

Since the mid-1950's, Quan Yin has transferred her guardianship as the Chohan of the Seventh Ray to Ascended Master Lord St. Germain and has fully focused her energy on preparing the ground for the arrival of the seventh ray souls. These are the souls who are collectively known as the Indigo children. They are called Indigo souls because their auric field carries the indigo — purple, magenta-blue colors — which are reflective of the Seventh Ray. These souls started pouring onto the Earth beginning around 1972, and each decade that followed has brought a greater number and more highly evolved souls to Earth.

In 2002, three decades later, Quan Yin and other Ascended Masters of Light informed us through channeling that practically every soul now being born is an indigo child. These souls are entering the planet from very bright and highly evolved star systems. This is why many of the new age literature call these new arrivals (mostly born since 1992) "the star children" or "the crystal children." These children are here to complete the evolution of Earth and finalize this circle of birth and death, helping us to enter into the Seventh Golden Age. That is why they are born on the SeventhRay — which is the last ray — to complete this cycle of seven (to read more on rays, see the chapter on Soul Lineage of Light). As the guardian — Chohan — of the Seventh Ray for 14,000 years, Quan Yin's focus has been on the Purple Ray and to assist in the return of the Divine Plan according to the original design. By restoring order on Earth, by transmuting pain and forgetfulness and through focus on Pure White Light of God unity, we will attain Mastery. The Purple Ray will transmute all differentiation and bring us back to unity in pure white light of the I AM. (I am preparing a book on Indigo children to go into print in 2006). In it, Quan Yin gives suggestions to parents of Indigo children and to the Indigo souls themselves. The oldest of these souls are now in their 30's. These Indigo adults are to be the leaders of our communities, nations and the world, leading us to God unity and finalizing this cycle of evolution of Earth to attain greater light.

Quan Yin has chosen the two qualities of compassion and mercy as her gift to the world because in her many lifetimes in physical embodiment (before her Ascension), those were the energies with which she worked. She has had many lifetimes on Earth as healer and teacher, sharing compassion and bestowing mercy upon humanity until she finally ascended. Since her Ascension she has been directing the rays and energies of mercy to the people of Earth. She offers her mercy to us. This mercy she has gained through the thousand years of service and focus on that ray — mercy. We will receive assistance directly from Quan Yin due to her intercession in our lives — not because of any merits that we have to earn but because of her intercession. She has already earned it and is willing to bring it into our lives. Something which would ordinarily take months or years to achieve if we are left on our own accord can be attained through her mercy in a matter of days or weeks. Her only condition is that we ask for her intercession and request that she would bestow her mercy and compassion upon us in all matters of our lives.

Having her statue or picture somewhere in your house, office, shop, on your work desk or on an altar helps to bring her energy into your life and is a great way to keep remembering to ask her intercession. Over the years, I have witnessed the amazing changes that happen to people as soon as Quan Yin comes into their lives. At relevant workshops and lectures, I try to make her pictures and statues available for purchase. This is for people who find the desire and urge to bring her physical presence into their lives through the symbology of her statue or pictures. I prayed and struggled for a long time before I found my first statue of her and, that made me even more determined to help find ways to bring her into people's lives. One of my greatest desires is that someday soon Quan Yin's name would be well known, and her image could be found in every household in the East, West, North, South and everywhere in between. For available items and further information on Quan Yin, visit www.nasrinsafai.com.

Return of the Kumaras

Commentary: Normally Orion represents to us the masculine energies, yet in this exercise we are greeted with the feminine forces here, the Seven Orionite Goddesses. Venus represents the feminine mother or sister energies to our Earth, and we are greeted by the Seven masculine Kumaras. This is for the balancing of the planetary male and female bodies. From our sister planet Venus we receive the Father energies of Sanat Kumara and the other Kumaras. From our brother planet Orion we receive the Goddess Mother energies of the Orionite Goddesses. In this discourse, Quan Yin lovingly and patiently explains and answers the following: What is the role of Orion? Who are the Kumaras? Who is the feminine principle? What is the purpose for anchoring of the pure white feminine ray of remembrance?

QUAN YIN, CHANNELED SEPTEMBER 10, 2002

My children of Light, I am Quan Yin.

I have offered to come on behalf of all the Masters. Take a deep breath as we set up a pillar of Light in the center of this circle. I call forth the legions of Michael to take their positions in all the directions creating a circle of Light. I call upon the Buddhas and bodhisattvas of compassion. I invite the Brotherhoods and the Sisterhoods of the White Lodge. I call upon the energies of Melchizedek. I call upon the energies of the Seven Kumaras, the Sanat Kumara, the Logos for your Earth, and all his brothers of light. I call upon the Masters and the Guardians of Venus. I call upon the energies and Masters of Jupiter. In our solar system,

Jupiter is our eldest brother from a spiritual planetary perspective. After the sun, which is our Father planet, Jupiter has the highest quotient of light. There is word amongst the higher realms of Light that the possibility exists in the future of our solar system that Jupiter may potentially evolve to become a sun, the second sun of our solar system, creating a binary system of suns. With two suns in our skies, we will never have to experience darkness again.

Ponder that for a moment. Yet don't let it carry you away too far. It is a thought in the mind of God, perhaps many, many hundreds of thousands, even millions of years away from where we are in the evolution of all the planetary bodies and our solar system. But then again, ponder this: time doesn't exist, everything is happening simultaneously and we are witnessing it right here, right now. After all, thoughts are things. Anything that we can think of is a thought that we have retrieved from the mind of God. If you can think it, you can manifest it, or it has already been done. Imagine that!

I would like to bring your attention to the energies of Orion. There is one specific planet — it is actually a star system — that is also very prominent in the life of Earth. There is an alignment that takes place with this star system and your Earth, actually with your solar system. And this alignment will assist in Wisdom being downloaded to the energy field of your planet. The energies of Wisdom are being offered to you from this specific star system. In time to come, I will introduce you to the beings — the guardians — of this star system.

The Kumaras and that specific star system in Orion have made a pact. The return of the Kumaras has been facilitated by the star system in Orion. The guardians in the star system in Orion are female beings, the leaders and the decision makers. The global guardians for that star system are female beings. The majority that sits on the board in that system are female, 75% female, 25% male. I tell you this because the feminine principle is coming forth.

The return of the Kumaras is going to be in the form of the feminine. Many thousands of years ago, the energies of the Kumaras were pulled away from the Earth. The Kumaras retrieved their energies from the Earthly realms. Their energies were lifted up to an etheric retreat in Upper Gobi Desert. Their physical bodies were taken to Venus to await this moment, the moment that is approaching now. As of midnight tonight (September 11, 2002), those energies will begin to penetrate into the atmosphere of Earth yet again. Why midnight? Because this is the time of a new alignment. The Kumaras will return to the Earth this time in feminine form. They will lower their energies back to the atmosphere of Earth through the feminine principle. They are receiving assistance from the star systems in Orion mainly because that system is activated and works with the feminine principle.

The two energies combined are of great benefit to Earth. In terms of realities that Earth beings could choose from, you have moved your quotient of Light to the highest possible degree. You have chosen the highest and best alternate reality to become your ultimate reality. (Note: The Masters have explained to us that there are many layers of parallel and alternate realities lying over each other. We choose from these according to our personal, group and planetary performance.) This pleases the Masters and the Guides and the Throne of Grace and the Throne of the Undifferentiated Source. Therefore there is a celebration going on in the higher realms.

Anchoring the Ray of Remembrance

To accomplish this journey I would like to ask that you gather four people, two male and two female, to anchor these energies. We have invited you to be the holders of this Light. Become consciously aware of this fact, and if you accept it we request that you maintain your awareness and consider yourselves standing each on a point of a square, two male and two female, totally balanced energies for the anchoring of this Light. (Note: Originally four people were called to receive these energies. If you wish to perform the ceremony, then gather three other people and take positions in the grid. To personally receive and digest these energies, you can do them alone.)

I ask that you begin by sounding nine Aums. Let us begin. Participants: *"Aum, Aum, Aum, Aum, Aum, Aum, Aum, Aum, Aum."*

We will now lower the energies down to you. You will feel the energies first through your crown chakra and it will begin moving down. The color range is in the blues. It is beginning to lower itself as we speak. It will penetrate your crown chakra moving down. You may first see the Light as pure white Light. It will then begin to spin in deep blue colors, very vibrant, moving down your body.

The next part of the body that will feel the impact of this new Ray of Light is your heart. And the name that

93

has been chosen for this ray of Light — I'll call this ray the Ray of Remembrance. There are many suggestions from the Board for the name. The simplest would be to call it the Ray of Remembrance. It is the remembrance of your own origin as Light, pure white Light. Pause and take a deep breath and feel the energies of the Ray of Remembrance working on your body and through you in the environment.

Pause and call the Ray of Remembrance to work on your body in the name of the I AM THAT I AM. The third part of your body that will feel these energies is your soul. Solar plexus is the seat of the soul. The last part of the body that you will feel these energies is the root chakra. Once it hits your root chakra, make sure you send it down your legs into the bottom of the feet and from there to the core crystal in the center of the Earth. Anchor the energies in the center of the Earth.

In recalling the Ray of Remembrance, become aware of the energies of the Kumaras, the Seven Kumaras. They have been the guardians of Earth, who have had to release their energies from Earth and who are returning now to reno-vate, reconstruct, to raise the quotient of Light to bring you to your original intent, to assist in spreading the original blueprint back on the grid system of Earth. This will allow you to receive through your bodies the energies of the Ray of Remembrance.

Begin sounding the Aum. Do this as loudly as you can. Do this exercise in Nature. Bring a favorite crystal to hold. Become aware of your surroundings. Become aware of the energies that move through your body. Become aware of nature and the plants. Make a conscious

94

intent that every object, every item, every soul, every consciousness, the consciousness of the five elements — the
Water, the Earth, the Fire, the Air and the Ethers — are
involved in this.

Pause and take a deep breath. Feel the energies of the
Ray of Remembrance working on your body and through
you in the environment. First feel the energies as they are
anchored in this immediate environment and through your
body. Then the energies move in waves from the center
where the four of you are located. They move through
everything in the space and spread in every which direction. Watch it spread. Watch it move through the crust of
the Earth to the core. Watch it spread over the crust all
around the Earth. From within to around the Earth and into
the Universe it vibrates, this Ray of Remembrance.

Come with me now while the awareness moves through
all objects to the core of the Earth and around the surface of
the Earth. While the anchoring will continue through your
bodies, moving to all places, people and things, come with me.

Now and forever, I am your mother, Quan Yin.

Quan Yin will continue on the next phase of this journey in the next chapter.

Merging With the Kumara of Your Soul Lineage

Commentary: Quan Yin says this is a healing for your
bodies, emotions, mind, soul and spirit. Let your spirit feel
the joy of this union. The specific color of the Initiation
Ray that is offered you is the ray for your own lineage.

(Note: That lineage remains the same through all the incarnations you have had on Earth plane. That connection remains strong from one incarnation to the next. You continue your work with that particular Kumara from your own essence and lineage whether you are consciously aware of it or not. Most of us are completely unaware and have forgotten that such an agreement exists between us.)

As you do become consciously aware however, you may begin to call upon your specific quality from the Ray of Remembrance and the assistance of the Kumara who is your guide. You may use this exercise and work with each of the Seven Kumaras individually at different times to receive further strength, assistance and greater remembrance of your own soul consciousness at planetary level on this Earth plane. This lineage is different from your soul lineage of light, the ray upon which you come to Earth. Each one of us comes to Earth upon one of the seven rays, which carries one quality with it of either will, wisdom, love, purity, truth, service or order. The planetary Ray of Remembrance offered by the Kumaras as our planetary logos relates to the act of service we perform in assisting the Kumaras' completion of the rescue mission for Earth and all souls' attainment of enlightenment.

QUAN YIN, CHANNELED SEPTEMBER 10, 2002

My children of light, I am Quan Yin.

First we will go to Shamballa. There we will meet the Kumaras. From there I will take you to the star system in Orion. We will meet the new guardians, the Queen of this planet. You will find your personal guardians, your personal guides in both of those places. These beings will assist you from this day on and will be very active in your lives. I request of you that you tune into their energies and that you hold on to those energies in total conscious awareness, specifically for the course of the next three months. By solstice in December (2002), these energies will have completed the course of their anchoring. Once the anchoring is complete, the Earth will shift to a new phase of evolution. (Note: Although the anchoring has been completed, as you read these words connect with the energies of it because your attention and your "will" helps to maintain and strengthen the cause.)

A new Light force will begin to shine on Earth. You will feel the energies of that Light force from this moment on in the crown chakra, in the heart, the solar plexus, in the root and in your feet. The sensation will be one of becoming lighter. You will feel less achiness. You will feel a lessening of any pain. You will feel a greater degree of hopefulness, joy in your hearts and a trust and knowing that everything is moving in a positive direction to Light and to the ultimate objective of God Unity.

Journey to Shamballa

From the point of Light where the Undifferentiated Source and I are One, I call upon the blueprint for the etheric Shamballa. From the Mind of God which holds the blueprint, I call upon the Threads of Light. I call upon the Threads of Light. I call upon the Threads of Light.

I request a dispensation for you to be given permission to move cocooned in the Threads of Light to the etheric

Shamballa to meet the Kumaras and receive guidance from them. To recognize the Kumara who is your personal guide in the etheric Shamballa, I request that your personal guide would merge and unite in oneness with you. Wrap yourself in the threads of light. Repeat seven times the sound of Aum (Om). Wrap yourself in the light and move as fast as you can. Taking the Threads of Light, being pulled into the energies of the etheric Shamballa, see yourself at the gateway of Light. There is an enormous gateway before you. It is made of pure golden Light. I command the doors of Shamballa to open up to this group of enlightened beings for their entry and for their initiation. I call forth the Ray of Remembrance to imbue every being as they set foot through the threshold of Light. The doors are open. Enter now. Pause inside. Take a deep breath.

You are greeted by the Seven Kumaras. They all wear ceremonial robes. They all hold scepters in their hands. They all wear crowns of gold. They wear capes of varying colors of maroon, magenta, deep dark fuschia, deep dark purple, deep dark Nile blue, deep dark maroon. Greet them. Stand before each one. Remember who you are. Move from one to the other. All seven you have worked with. All seven you have known. Let the memory banks download the codes. Let your mind receive. Pause. Take a deep breath. Remember them. Recall the memories of your knowing.

I would like to request a merging with each of the Kumaras. Rather than calling them by name, I will call upon the ray and its color. Allow yourself to receive the specific Kumara. As they stand before you and they extend their energies to you, you will find that you become one with them as their energy force field penetrates into yours, merging and uniting as one.

First I will call upon the Kumara that comes on the deep fuschia pink ray. Feel the energetic force field before you. The energy begins to move into your body. Receive it. Allow the memories to return to you. While you are in the force field of this Kumara I call upon the deep blue Ray of Remembrance, and I ask that your beingness be imbued by the energies of the Ray of Remembrance. Feel the Kumara of deep fuschia pink ray. Pause and receive. Feel the healing forces of this Kumara's vibration. Pause for a moment and feel your body imbued with the Kumara's deep fuschia pink ray. The Kumara retrieves the energies from your body. You know that you have received a blessing. Take a deep breath and absorb the blessings you have received.

Second in line is the deep, deep purple. The Kumara stands before you. Deep purple energies vibrate from the essence of the Kumara entering and merging into your body. Deep, deep purple, the purple color of the petunias, vibrant, merging and uniting. I call forth the Ray of Remembrance to download the memories to your body and your essence. Pause and receive. Take a deep breath and allow the deep dark petunia purple ray of this Kumara penetrate and heal your body and your being. As the Kumara retrieves the energies back into his body, know that you have received a blessing. Take a deep breath and absorb the blessings you have received.

The third ray is a deep magenta color. It is a purple mixed with red. As the Kumara stands before you, the vibration of the magenta ray penetrates through your essence.

Bathe in those energies as I call forth the Ray of Remembrance to download the memories for the remembrance to return to your essence. Pause and receive. Take a deep breath and meditate, receiving the magenta purple ray of remembrance from this Kumara. Allow it to bathe and heal your entire beingness. As the Kumara retrieves the energies, you have received the blessing. Take a deep breath and absorb the blessings you have received.

The fourth Kumara is a deep, dark maroon color. As you stand receiving the vibration of the deep, dark maroon, I call forth the Ray of Remembrance to imbue your energy field and to bring forth the memories of your own origin and the downloading of your memory banks. Pause and receive. Take a moment to meditate on the deep, dark maroon aspect of the Ray of Remembrance offered to you by this Kumara. Bathe and heal all the body, mind, emotions, spirit and soul in these energies. Pause and receive. You are nurtured and healed through the vibration of this ray. The Kumara retrieves the energies and you have received the blessing. Take a deep breath and absorb the blessings you have received.

The fifth Kumara is a deep blue color, a very vibrant blue. It is not a dark one but it is a deep one. It is a dense blue color but vibrant in nature; it is condensed and very vibrant. I call forth the Ray of Remembrance. The color of the Ray of Remembrance is very similar to the essence of this Kumara. Download the energies of healing through the Ray of Remembrance. Pause and receive. Take a deep breath and be filled with the loving deep blue healing energies of this Kumara. Feel your entire beingness healed and brought to wholeness from this encounter. As this Kumara retrieves the energies, you receive the blessing. Take a deep breath and absorb the blessings you have received.

The sixth Kumara carries a ray also of blue color but this one is a deep, dark color much like Nile blue. The energies vibrate out of its essence into yours and I call upon the Ray of Remembrance. The downloading of the force field takes place. Pause and receive. Breathe into your cell structure, your essence and your entire being the nile blue ray, the power of the remembrance ray offered by this Kumara. Feel the healing energies pour through you. As the Kumara retrieves the energies, you receive a great blessing and healing. Take a deep breath and absorb the blessings you have received.

The last of the Kumaras also carries a very deep, dark blue color like the dark of the night. It almost borders on black but it is not black. It is a very dark blue color and yet extremely vibrant and very potent. As you stand receiving the vibration, it is the deepest and most penetrating of all the energies. I call forth the Ray of Remembrance and I ask for the downloading of the memory banks. Pause and receive. Fill your soul, spirit, heart, mind, body, emotions, and being with this last of the Kumaras' most intense dark blue, vibrant and full of potent light. Completely imbue your own being in this light and feel encapsulated inside. As the Kumara retrieves the energies, you have received the final blessing. Take a deep breath and absorb the blessings you have received.

Take your time. Return to your own essence. Greet and bless each one individually. Merge and unite as you stand before them. Once you greet all seven, one will take you to the Initiation Chamber. Pause and take a deep breath. Prepare for your initiation.

Now follow to the Initiation Chamber the one Kumara that walks before you. (Note: One of the Masters will be your guide. If you feel drawn to a specific Kumara, then follow that one. If not, you may choose from the list above.) This is a healing for your bodies, emotions, mind, soul and spirit. Let your spirit feel the joy of this union. The specific color of the Initiation Ray which is offered to you is the ray for your own lineage.

Whenever you need assistance, you may call upon this ray and the specific color that brings you healing. The Kumara who has taken you into the Initiation Chamber is the head of this lineage. The return of the Kumaras brings the remembrance of the seven threads of the lineage back to you. Pause for a long moment and bathe in the initiation ceremony and the energies. In the initiation chamber you receive from the heart and the third eye of the Kumara a beam of light that emanates to your own heart and third eye. This awakens the memories of your own lineage of light and contract of service, or your divine mission, for which you have incarnated into human body. Absorb these energies and offer yourself in service.

It is time to depart now. Let us together return to the main hall. Let us thank and bless what we have received, as the one Kumara who has initiated you will take you from this point to the star system in the constellation Orion.

Now and forever, I am your mother, Quan Yin.

Orion: Initiation by the Feminine Principle

QUAN YIN, CHANNELED SEPTEMBER 12, 2002

My children of Light, I am Quan Yin.

From the point of Light where the Undifferentiated Source and I are One, I call upon the original blueprint for the elevation of Light to meet and unite with our own origin and our own essence in the specific star in the constellation Orion that has been prepared to receive us. In the company of the Kumaras we travel. Take a deep breath and pause. From the Mind of God which holds the blueprint, I call forth the Thread of Light. In the company of the Kumara, cocoon yourself in the Thread of Light. The filaments are all around you. You are pulled through the time-space continuum to the atmosphere of this planet. Take a deep breath and pause.

Become aware of the sky. Become aware of the structures. They are very different from what you are familiar with. You have journeyed to this spot once before consciously. You do journey occasionally in dreamtime. Lately you have been journeying to this place frequently in dreamtime. Observe the surroundings. We are at the gateway of Light. Sound "Aum" out loud seven times.

The gateway is open. There is an entourage of seven female beings in robes that you might call priestess ceremonial robes. Become aware of the headdress. It looks like the filaments of Light with pearls and other vibrant gemstones around the headdress. Become aware of their faces. They are very pointed. Become aware of their eyes. They are extra large by your standards. Become aware of

103

their bodies; they are made of semi-form, not as dense as the bodies that you have. They can hold a much greater quotient of light than your dense bodies can.

You can recognize the hierarchy of their positions by the vibration of their headdress. Their headdress is their signature of Light. If you look at their headdresses, some of them are vibrating a larger and more intense vibration halo of Light. The colors also vary. The greater the colors emanating from their headdress, the higher their level of seniority. The color vibrates outward like a halo. One amongst the seven will accompany you to the Initiation Chamber. Upon entry into the Initiation Chamber you are requested to stand on a platform of Light. Below your feet there is a circle of Light. When you take your position on that platform, a pillar of Light is illuminated. Pause and take a deep breath. Receive the energies.

The energy is almost electric. The vibration of the energy is more of an electrical nature. Because this planet is held through the vibrational force field of a majority of female beings, they can work with electrical forces. Since those electrical forces are masculine by nature, this brings a balance. The female beings themselves hold a great degree of magnetic force within them. From the merging of the two there is a balancing of the electromagnetic force fields.

As you stand under the pillar of Light and it is illuminated, the force field around you begins to expand and the charge begins to increase. It is somewhat like an electric shock but pleasant sensations rather than painful ones. When the intensity of the charge has reached the maximum that your body can receive, the female being who is your guide will join inside the pillar and merge with you. Notice the color vibration that this guide is sending out to you. The color of the ray given to you corresponds to the seven rays that are being sent to the Earth by this star system. Pause and receive the charge, hold it with you and meditate to fully absorb all its potential. Repeat this exercise to receive greatest benefits from it.

Now and forever, I am your mother, Quan Yin.

Follow with the next exercise.

Unlimited Light and Healing for All Kingdoms

QUAN YIN, CHANNELED SEPTEMBER 12, 2002

My children of Light, I am Quan Yin.

Through the combined energies of the seven female beings and the Seven Kumaras, a balanced electromagnetic force is brought to the Earth for the purpose of the elevation of Light and an increase in the quotient of Light. All the old criteria regarding how much Light you can hold within your dense bodies are no longer applicable. Through this new system of vibration you will shed the density and acquire a new lightness. This is a great healing tool. You can use these vibrations to heal your bodies, heal each other, heal people, places and things. You can charge your crystals with this healing vibration. You can cleanse the waters of the earth with this healing vibration. You can bring balance and equilibrium returning to the original intent for all souls. You can hold that intention for Earth and all creation.

Let every molecule, every cell, every iota of your being absorb these energies. Don't hold back. This is the ultimate healing presented to you. The energy of this healing will begin pouring onto Earth as of midnight tonight (entering 9/11/02). It will absorb to itself and transmute all negative energies. All difficult emotions can be released. All fear can be absorbed, transmuted and returned to Light through these balanced vibrations. All feelings of separation can be released.

For your own healing purpose, as you stand in this pillar of Light, request and intend that all fear be removed — past, present and future — from your body and your beingness. Any and all emotions that you wish to release, any and all concerns that no longer serve you, give it all up now. Offer it up and let it go. Now is the time.

Now, on your behalf, I call upon the energies of trust and acceptance. I ask on your behalf that the energies of trust in Light, surrender to Light, acceptance of Light, healing through the Light to be brought to your bodies and your beingness: Trust, surrender, heal, accept. Now do this for your loved ones: Trust, surrender, acceptance and healing. Now do it for the Planet: Trust, surrender, acceptance and healing. Now do it for the collective consciousness of the masses: Trust, surrender, acceptance and healing. Now do it for the plants, the minerals, the animals: Trust, surrender, acceptance and healing. Now do it for the bodies of water: Trust, surrender, acceptance and healing. Now do it for the element of Earth: Trust, surrender, acceptance and healing. Now do it for the element of Fire: Trust, surrender, acceptance and healing. Now do it for the element of Air and all anger that the element of Air has been working with to be released and transmuted.

May the winds of the world come to peace and harmony with all other elements; Trust, surrender, acceptance and healing. Now do it for the spirit of all things: Trust, surrender, acceptance and healing. For the physical bodies of all things: Trust, surrender, acceptance and healing. For the emotional bodies of all things: Trust, surrender, acceptance and healing. For the mental bodies of all things: Trust, surrender, acceptance and healing. For the etheric bodies of all things: Trust, surrender, acceptance and healing. For all body systems: Trust, surrender, acceptance and healing. For all levels and layers of all bodies: Trust, surrender, acceptance and healing.

Now we move to the energy of service. Let healing come, bringing forth the unfoldment of the path of Light upon which each individual present here will walk in Service. Pause. It is complete. Take a deep breath.

The pillar of Light begins to dim and retreat its energies. The feminine being of Light retreats her vibration and moves out of the pillar, and you begin to step away from the circle. We leave the Initiation Chamber in the company of the feminine guide, returning to the main hall. Greeting and blessing the seven feminine creative essences that represent the seven consorts to the seven Kumaras, we bless and thank all that has been received. Returning through the gate of Light, we call forth the filaments of Light. From the Mind of God I call forth the Thread of Light. If you so wish it, request that the guiding Kumara and the guiding feminine essence continue on the journey of Light with you for as long as necessary for the anchoring of these energies and for all that can be learned and exchanged through this experience.

Return to your physical bodies. Take a deep breath. We come back with great joy from this journey of Light, through the star systems, through the constellation of Orion, back to the etheric Shamballa, offering joy and gratitude for what we have received. Remaining inside the force field of the Thread of Light, I bring you back to your physical bodies. The two guides stay with you. Remain in awareness of their presence with you at all times. Pause and take a deep breath.

Take this opportunity and learn from it. As you retire to bed tonight, request their presence and their guiding Light to take you to those realms and dimensions of reality where learning and understanding can be brought to you. Request that the doors of the Temples of Wisdom, Knowledge and Understanding be open to you in the company of the guides. Request that the learning begins and continues until the ultimate goal is attained, serving the path of Light, stepping up the quotient of Light, walking on the journey of homebound to Light, attaining Light, becoming Light, fully immersed in Light, as Light.

Pure Light I AM.
Point of Light I AM.
White Light I AM.
Bright Light I AM.
Light I AM.
I AM. I AM. I AM.

So it is. It is done. I bless you in the company of all the Masters and Mistresses of Light who celebrate your victory at this grand moment, at this turning point, at this fateful moment of turning full force in the direction of Light. I love you. I hold you dear to my own heart. I will continue to pray for your joyful return journey on the Path of Light. Now and forever, I am your Mother, Quan Yin.

Visiting Venusian Temples of Wisdom in Dreamtime

Commentary by Quan Yin: Temples of wisdom and knowledge within the planetary field of Venus have been activated to receive you during these times of energy exchange between Earth and Venus. Those of you who have offered yourself in service visit these temples in dreamtime.

QUAN YIN, CHANNELED FEBRUARY 13, 2004.

My children of light, I am Quan Yin.

Your physical body remains here on Earth. At dreamtime, your consciousness leaves your body to receive teachings in the etheric palaces on Venus. Because of all these activities, at times you may desire to eat food that would ground you or food that you don't normally crave. If you find yourself craving sugary foods, grounding foods; if you are binging, or you are hungry for no reason at all, this is your body's way to keep you here. If you feel that you are bloated, bigger than you normally are and it is not a comfortable feeling for you, remember that it has to be this way in order for you to be able to pulse into and out of different time-space continuums.

Energetically, you are connecting to Venus. A time tunnel of light has been created for you to connect your physical body here on Earth to your etheric body which is receiving energy in the palaces and retreats on Venus.

You have heard of the palace of Shamballa. There are inner chambers inside of the palace of Shamballa, which are for the most adept of the initiates, for the highly evolved initiates. These inner chambers are where you are taken.

If you find yourself energetically attracted to the colors and energies of emerald green, that is a natural phenomenon resulting from the above experience. It will be very beneficial for you to wear emeralds if you have any. If you don't have any emeralds, then try and find a piece of raw emerald (which is less expensive) or a good quality piece of jade that you can wear at all times. If you have a piece of emerald, even though it is in with other gems, it is very good for you to wear it. If you do not feel comfortable wearing it out, put it in a pouch and wear it around your neck under your clothes. Then you will be with the energies of instant manifestation and precipitation. Precipitation meaning manifesting from thin air, because this is what is happening to you.

In one moment energetically you are pulsing somewhere where your body isn't, but an etheric body has been prepared for you to receive the energies. Remember that this too shall pass. As you extend and expand your quotient of light and receive the teachings and all the beneficial energies from these temples, you will graduate and move to higher realms of light for other acts of service and to receive greater knowledge and wisdom. In the process, your bodies will adjust to the new energies. Once fully adjusted, life will bring you new adventures and explorations to expand your mind, body, soul, spirit and emotions.

So it is. Now, as always, I am your mother, Quan Yin.

Minerva

Introduction

Elohim Minerva is the feminine aspect and consort to Cassiopia. Together Cassiopia and Minerva are in charge of the illumination of the divine plan put forth and the necessary qualities for bringing the perception of the design into manifestation. The seven pairs of the Mighty Elohim are the grand architects of our entire creation.

In the literature of Summit Lighthouse, the Elohim are described as such:

"Elohim are the powerful beings who head up the builders of creation branch of cosmic hierarchy. Elohim is one of the Hebrew names of God. It is a uni-plural noun referring to the twin flames of the Godhead that comprise the "Divine Us." When speaking specifically of either the masculine or feminine half, the plural form is retained because both halves contain the divine whole. Elohim preside over the creation of star systems, planets and all physical life evolving anywhere in the universe. They carry the greatest concentration and highest vibration of light that we can comprehend." (see www.tsl.org/Elohim)

Because the Elohim hold the highest vibration of light they are residents of very high dimensions of reality close to the Throne of God and in close proximity to the Undifferentiated Source, which is God before form. To come to lower dimensions of reality requires great concentration and great sacrifice on their part. Our present world of third dimensional reality is too dense and too polluted for beings of the Elohim, who are beings of high intensity light. By the same token, to hold their energy inside of a body in order to channel their message is quite a challenge.

Elohim Minerva has given messages through me a few times, but unfortunately the recording equipment has not been able to cope with her high intensity, and most of her messages have not been recorded. Fortunately I can present to you a sampling of her energies from a recording which did produce results. This was a very auspicious ceremony to finalize our workshop series on the teachings of alchemy given by Master Thoth. (Refer to the Thoth chapter).

I have always felt a closeness to the presence of the Elohim Minerva, and yet I was surprised that she would choose to come forward since her male consort Cassiopia is much more commonly heard of in the available literature. In researching the available material I found out that Goddess Minerva was the Roman name of Goddess Athena, and a large body of literature exists from both the Greek and Roman times from Minerva and Athena.

In Greek history, Minerva is also known as Pallas Athena. In *Man-His Origin, History, and Destiny* by Werner Schroeder, Pallas Athena is mentioned as:
> *"Pallas Athena, Goddess of Truth, was high priestess at the Temple of Truth. The pilgrims would visit her to gain from the magnetizing effect of the green flame of truth." (p. 49)*

I have given a more extensive explanation of the scope and qualities of Elohim Minerva and her consort as well as all other Mighty Elohim in the chapter on Soul Lineage of Light.

Minerva: Prayers and Journeys

Commentary: This discourse was given as the final session of a workshop series. The group sat around a circle with large crystals positioned behind each member and candles lit in the center. All these crystal grids were set to anchor the energies of Elohim Minerva and all the gifts that she bestowed upon us through the journey. This was the first time I channeled Goddess Minerva in a large group setting. If you look at the date of this discourse you will notice that it was given to us at the 21st year anniversary of the Harmonic Convergence. I have explained the significance of the Harmonic Convergence in the following pages where Elohim Minerva refers to it.

MINERVA, CHANNELED JULY 21, 2003

Beloved of the light, I am Minerva. Take a deep breath with me.

From the space of your solar plexus call upon your soul. From the space of your heart call upon your heart flame. From the space of your thymus call upon your spirit. From the space of your throat and your third eye, call upon the mind. Allow me to take you with these four aspects together through the silver-golden cord, the antahkarana, up through the crown chakra. Notice the rainbow colored light as you move through your own crown chakra. Notice the cylinder of light, pure white light, and golden light that is formed around your head and your body, as we move the spirit, the soul, the heart and the mind on a journey upward through the cylinder of golden white light. We reach up to the throne of the Undifferentiated Source. Upon arrival, we meet and merge with the presence of the I AM THAT I AM.

Repeat: *"From the space of light in the heart of the Undifferentiated Source, I am one with the mighty perfected presence of the I AM THAT I AM."* Say this three times and take a deep breath. Pause and take a deep breath. Prepare yourself to be engulfed with the light of the I AM. Envision the presence of the Elohim Minerva standing over you, towering with her arms outstretched, pouring out the energies of the light of wisdom upon you. Say the following invocation: *"From the space of light in the heart of the Undifferentiated Source I AM one with the mighty Perfected Presence of the I AM THAT I AM. From the space of light in the heart of the Undifferentiated Source I am the mighty Perfected Presence of the I AM THAT I AM."*

On behalf of the united perfected aspect of everyone's soul, spirit, mind and heart I invoke the mighty perfected presence of the I AM THAT I AM to embody and imbue the spirit, the soul, the mind and the heart for everyone, creating a spirited, soulful, mindful, heartful entity of light. From that space of light I invoke my consort Cassiopia. From that space of light I invoke Cyclopea, I invoke Pacifica, I invoke Crystal, I invoke Angelica, I invoke Orion, Hercules, Arcturus, Purity, Peace, Astrea. (Note: Minerva and her consort Cassiopia are the Elohim of the Second Ray, Illumination. All the others are the Elohim of other rays. For a full description, see the chapter on Soul Lineage of Light).

I invoke the hosts of the ascended masters. I invoke the great cosmic beings of light. I invoke the crystalline structures to begin humming and singing to the glory of the I AM THAT I AM . (Note: Minerva is referring to a crystal grid we had set up around the room with very large crystals, mostly selenite towers weighing more than 50 pounds, to guard and bring energy from the four directions, as well as smaller varieties of crystals placed around a circle behind every member of the group.)

I invoke cosmic light to pour upon this group. I invoke the cosmic beings of light to come forward. I invoke the gates of light from the constellation Orion to open its gateways and to pour the light of the feminine principle upon Earth and upon humanity, anchoring the energy upon the grid that we now have set in this holy, blessed spot.

I demand all darkness to be released from this spot, all obstacles to be released from this spot, anyone, anything who has malintention directed at this spot. And everyone who visits this spot will receive ten-fold their intentions in return. Anyone, anything that brings their love and light to this spot will receive ten-fold their intentions in return. I clear the energies for only light of the purest and the brightest vibration to vibrate in this spot now and forever. I invoke the purest and the brightest of light to ignite the spark of God Unity in the hearts of every individual member of this group, anyone who has ever been touched by the members of this group, anyone who will ever be touched by the members of this group.

And the group entity that is formed, I hold this group entity sacred and holy. I imbue the entity of this group and every individual member with the Seven-Fold Flame of Creation. The Seven-Fold Flame consists of the seven flames that hold the fire of life within the seven rays. This entire world is created through the manifest essence of the seven rays. Each soul comes from one of the seven rays. Even countries and continents come to existence upon one of the seven rays. Which ray souls represent depends on their soul lineage or their lineage of light. Envision a crown in the form of the Seven-Fold Flame is now placed upon your heads. From the space of light where the Undifferentiated Source and I are one, I call forth the Throne of Grace to be lowered upon this spot. I invoke the gateways of light from the constellation Arcturus to open up.

From the space of light where the Undifferentiated Source and I are one, I invoke the purest and brightest light to ignite the Flame of God Unity in the hearts of every member of this group and ignite the Seven-Fold Flame on the crown chakra of every member of this group. I hold this entity sacred and holy. I hold this ground sacred and holy. This ground is protected now and forever from all harm. From the space of light where the Undifferentiated Source and I are one, I call upon the energies of the constellation Sirius to open up and pour out their light to this grid that we are about to form in this spot and carry in the hearts of each person as well as in the heartcore of the group entity that is formed from this communion. I invoke the Throne of Grace to bless this grid.

I invoke the Throne of the Undifferentiated Source to bless this grid. I invoke the Sisterhoods and the Brotherhoods of the White Lodge, the holy hosts of the Ascended Masters and Mistresses of Light, gods and goddesses,

Mighty Elohim in all their aspects, in all their forms, in all their qualities. I AM THAT I AM, love I AM, bliss I AM, light I AM, ecstasy I AM, Blazing Fire of White Flame I AM, Blazing Fire of White Flame I AM, Blazing Fire of White Flame I AM. I call upon the hosts of Archangel Michael. I call upon the hosts of Lady Faith. I call upon the hosts of Archangel Jophiel. I call upon the hosts of Archangel Azriel. I call upon the hosts of Archangel Raphael. I call upon the hosts of Archangel Zadkiel. I call upon the hosts of Archangel Sandalphon. I call upon the hosts of Archangel Gabriel. I call upon the hosts of Archangel Uriel. I call upon the Seraphim, the Cherubim. I call upon the light of the angelic, archangelic, seraphic and cherubic light to come forth and to prepare the grounds for the Ascension of Earth Mother, for the awakening of the multitudes and the masses.

At this point I invoke you to go in your hearts and offer your personal intentions before I take you up on a journey. Ask for your intentions for this specific ceremony, ask for your personal intentions: whatever you wish to ask for. And ask for a group intention: peace and harmony on Earth, light to shine upon Earth, joy to reside in the hearts of all souls, peace and Brotherhood and Sisterhood of Light to reign on Earth. State your intentions. Take a deep breath. State your wishes and desires and offer up whatever you would like to offer. Pause and meditate in these energies.

Follow with the next phase as Minerva takes us to our sister planet Venus, the home of the Kumaras and the palace of Shamballa.

Journey to Venus, Orion, Arcturus and Sirius

Commentary: Shamballa is the heaven on Earth in which God originally intended humankind to reside. Humanity lost its state of purity and innocence, and the energies of Shamballa were retrieved from Earth and moved to the etheric planes in higher realms. As we begin to open our hearts again to truth, purity and innocence we will become ready to receive Shamballa back on Earth again. Goddess Minerva/Elohim Minerva is taking us to Venus where Shamballa presently resides. Shamballa is the home of the Seven Kumaras, the seven cosmic beings who work directly with the spiritual growth and evolution of earth and humankind. One of these great cosmic beings is Sanat Kumara.

MINERVA, CHANNELED JULY 21, 2003

Beloved of the Light, I am Minerva. Take a deep breath with me.

Come with me now through the tunnel of light, the golden white light. We will take a journey, first to Venus, visiting with the great beings of Shamballa to receive the keys to unlock the gateways of light. We then will journey to Orion, Arcturus and Sirius before our return journey back to Earth.

The object of this exercise is to take our plea to the Karmic Board. We request that the Brotherhoods and Sisterhoods of Light, the energies of white light, ascended beings of white light and the cosmic beings of white light come to the rescue of Earth and humanity and take Earth and humanity to the next level of evolution. By the force of our decrees and demands, by the force of our requests and asking, by the force of us knocking on the door, the doors shall be opened and the floodgates of light shall be given to Earth and humankind.

This harmonic convergence (August 16, 2003) will be the coming to fruition of the past 21 years of light. The first Harmonic Convergence was in 1987. The occasion was that a plea went out from the consciousness of humankind for help and assistance to be given to the multitude and masses of Earth beings and to the planet. Our brothers and sisters from the Ascended realms also known as the Masters of Light came from the four corners of the universe to help bring light and tilt the balance in favor of light. This is why Masters of Light such as Christ Maitreya have taken physical form. Other beings even at cosmic levels of light are coming to help. The Elohim and the Sanat Kumara are among them. It will be the culmination. It will be the reaching of spiritual adulthood. It will be the coming of age. In this process of coming of age, we will bring the energies of our elder brothers and sisters of light through Venus, which is our closest (almost a twin) planet, and from there Orion, Arcturus and Sirius, back to Earth.

Through the tunnel of light we weave our way as a group entity moving in spiral fashion, calling upon the energies of Ascended Mistresses and Masters of Light. I call forth all Seven Mighty Elohim and seven consorts, the Seven-Fold Flame, the Ascended Masters of Light, the great Master Thoth, the great Goddess of Victory (she has been victorious for over two hundred thousand years). The great Goddess of Liberty (in charge of liberating worlds and planets as well as countries, her energy vibrates through the statue of Liberty in Staton Island, New York). The great Divine

Mother of Light, the Cosmic Female Principle of Existence, the Cosmic Christ Heart Light, the blue Cross of Fire, the blue Sword of Mercy, the blue Flame of Mercy, the white-blazing Flame of Ascension, the golden Flame of God Unity.

We enter the palace of Shamballa. In the central hallway in the palace there are records of a civilization on Earth 250,000 years ago. It is for the decoding of the memory banks regarding this civilization that we are creating this group energy. We are here to retrieve the records of this civilization which has been the most significant and the most successful, the one with greatest light in the recent history of Earth. It is the blueprint of this civilization that we will retrieve and carry in our hearts on our journey to Orion to receive a blessing and an elevation from the Mother Goddess energies. From there to Arcturus to receive the wisdom and knowledge of the Wise Men, the masculine energy. And then to Sirius to receive the child energies, the female child energies. And this triune aspect, this trinity, we will bring back to Earth.

We will superimpose this reality upon the reality we have lived on Earth so far. By this work greater light shall shine upon Earth, and the old blueprint that has become so tarnished and polluted and full of disasters will then merge and unite in light, and then dissolve itself into the new blueprint of light. This is the purpose of this ceremony of light that we are performing now as a group entity. It is the blueprint of this new trinity of light that we will bring back as the God Flame inside our hearts with the help of the mother energies from Orion, the father energies from Arcturus and the child energies from Sirius.

In the center of the Palace of Shamballa, there is an altar in the form of a crescent moon. The crescent moon itself is made of mother of pearl. Behind it, there is a pillar the shape of a cylinder. This pillar of light is made of selenite crystal. At the very edge of each end of the crescent moon there are two large linghams. The lingham is the symbol of creation: it is the egg of life, it is the phallus, it is the womb. It is the triune aspect in itself: in the form of the egg that is inside the womb it represents the child, in the form of the phallus it represents the father. In the form of the yoni or the circle that holds the phallus within itself and holds the egg within its womb, it represents the mother energies. A shaft of blue light begins vibrating, illuminating the two linghams at the edge of the crescent moon. The linghams will begin to hum a tune.

Each one of you standing in the center of a stage at the depth of the crescent of the moon will find your own Twin Flame (the male or female consort or counterpart — the being that makes us complete and unites with us in oneness bringing final union) facing you. Hold your hands palms out and touch your Twin Flame at the palms. Look into each other's eyes.

When you make the connection with one another, the two of you will be teleported through a golden pillar of light to the civilization 250,000 years ago which was located on the land in what is now known as Siberian Desert. At that time it was a beautiful continent with Mediterranean Sea type of weather. For those of you who are now experiencing this civilization, feel your own bodies, see your own consort, your Twin Flame, in the body that he or she occupied in that time. See the crystalline temple structure. We will have to go into that structure in order to receive the blueprint. Those of you who wish to receive the blueprint find your way (glide) to that crystalline structure. It is an opaque crystalline structure. You will know how to enter. Pause. Take a deep breath. Compose your thoughts. Put your intention on finding yourself inside the structure and you will be there.

Once you enter you will see a very similar hallway, a crescent moon-shaped altar with two linghams at the edges. In the center, in front of the pillar of selenite, you will see a crystalline bowl, a singing bowl. It is very, very large. When you look inside of it, you blow the breath of light into it and it begins to hum. The ball begins to sing. From the sound vibration, the walls of the temple which are made of crystalline structures, begin to hum. Lights in profusion of colors will begin to emanate from every direction, penetrating your body and your being. Feel it in your heart. Feel it in your soul. Feel it in your spirit. Feel it in your mind. Receive the perfection of this blueprint as it downloads through the light and sound spectrum into your body, your mind, your spirit and soul. The decoding of the memories of this civilization and your role in it will continue for another 36 hours from now. You may continue to have flashbacks of the knowledge, the wisdom and the information. The most important quality of this race was their wisdom, and this is the reason why the Elohim of Wisdom, Cassiopia and Minerva, are in charge of this civilization. The illumination of light that emanated from this civilization beams throughout the entire Universe, the wisdom of the ages. As the lights begin to fade, let us offer a prayer of thanksgiving before we begin our journey to Orion.

Take a deep breath. Pause and Meditate. Absorb the energies and put out the intention that you receive and absorb all the wisdom and knowledge that will benefit you and the entire human race from this exercise over the next 36 hours or longer, whatever is the highest wisdom and in service to the light. Take a deep breath.

And continue with the next phase.

The Mother, Father and Dolphin Child: The Cosmic Christ Grid

MINERVA, CHANNELED JULY 21, 2003

Beloved of the light, I am Minerva. Take a deep breath with me.

Together now as a group, with each one of you in the company of your Twin Flame, stand in the same formation facing each other. Hold the palms touching one another, and in the center of the stage the golden white pillar of light will begin beaming to each one of you. And together we are teleported to the center of the constellation Orion, to the star system we know as Orionis.

Upon entry through the gateway of the temple in the city of Oriana we are greeted by the Seven Mighty Cosmic Beings of Light, the seven aspects of the Feminine Principle of Existence. One out of the seven is closest in lineage to your own. That one vibrates a certain shade of light that pulls you to her vibration. Let her take you by the hand to the inner chamber inside. She will stand with you and your Twin Flame forming a triangle. You will hold your palms out and reach for one another, both male and female aspects looking into her eyes. And the emanation of that

123

particular shade of light that she is vibrating begins to illumine the entire room and fill every cell, every molecule, every iota, every electron of your bodies and your beings — yourself and your Twin Flame.

As the shaft of light spins, you begin to see the genetic coding of the structure of the DNA that is downloaded into your bodies and your beings. The golden key of light is placed in the cosmic heart chakra. The formation of this golden key is a symbol. That symbol is the signature of your own lineage of light. The shape of the key that is placed in your cosmic heart is the symbol that is the signature of your own lineage of light, your emblem of light.

Once complete, the three of you together (you, your twin flame and the feminine cosmic being) begin spinning and merging in oneness, moving into a spiral of light, spinning outwards, out of Oriana, out of Orionis, in the direction of constellation Arcturus. In the center of this constellation there is the Arc, the star system of Arc; the capital city of Arctur is the gateway of entering. Beams of light emanating from the combined forces of the group will open up the temple doorways.

In the center of the great hallway, there is another similar altar. Seven male beings of light robed in ceremonial costumes have lined up. Each one is emanating a certain vibration of light. You are called to one. In the company of the Cosmic Feminine Principle from Orion you will follow the wise being of Arcturus to an inner chamber. In the center there is a shaft of light. You stand, four of you, beaming light to one another: the great cosmic being from Orion, the great cosmic being from Arcturus, the male and the female

— you and your consort — will form a diamond of light holding palms to each other. A vibration of light begins emanating from the heart of the wise male cosmic being. The emanation meets the same emanations from the heart of the feminine aspect, mixing and merging in oneness. These emanations reach up to your heart, to your soul, to your spirit and to your mind.

A key is formed, a symbol, a signature, a sign. This key is now placed in the center of your heart. See now the decoding upon the strands of DNA, and formation of new strands superimposed upon the old strands, affecting the structure of cells, molecules electrons, protons, neutrons and every iota of your being. The blueprint for the male aspect is now downloaded. As the shaft of light recedes back into the heart of the cosmic being from Orion and the cosmic being from Arcturus, the four of you begin spinning and spiraling, leaving this blessed inner chamber and enter into the spiral of light, moving in the direction of constellation Sirius.

We will journey to planet Sirius B, where the entire surface of the planet is covered with water. Upon your arrival, on the shores you can see the sand beneath your feet. The water is shallow. You can stand comfortably in it. The four of you, the Orionite, the Arcturian, you and your consort will await the child being of light in the form of a dolphin to arrive. The energy of the child aspect is held in the physical embodiment of these dolphins. When the flock of dolphins arrives you will spot the child that is the completion of your own cycle. Following that one dolphin, all four of you will enter in the water going deeper and deeper into the depths of the water until you reach the dark waters of the depth of the sea. Entering into a cave, suddenly all is illuminated in light. Swimming into this cave, above you see crystalline structures, formations much like clusters of amethyst, clusters of fluorite, clusters of rose colored, citrine colored, emerald colored crystalline structures. All the seven colors of the rainbow are represented. As you weave your way from one cave of crystalline light to another, beams of light emanate from the crystalline structures to all five of you: the Orionite, the Arcturian, you, your consort and the child dolphin. Finally, you come to a great hall where the domes emanate rose-pink colored light. At the center there is a floating stage. You are helped to stand on this stage. A great, pure white light silhouette of a human being appears at the center. This is the Elohim of Illumination.

The gift of the Elohim is to impregnate the womb of Mother Earth by placing the key in your heart. If you so wish to receive this key, give permission to the male/female aspect of the Elohim of Creation, Elohim of Illumination. They offer the key to you and download the blueprint for the perfected DNA structure for the new feminine child aspect in the center of your own cosmic heart. As the shafts of light begin emanating with greater intensity, from the touch of the hand of the Elohim you feel the light in your heart, you feel the light emanated into your body. The sounds of angelic singing emanate from the walls of the cave. Dolphins all around you chirp and sing with joy from this union. The work is now complete.

Touch the heart of the cosmic being from Orion in thanksgiving as she touches our hearts. We touch the heart of the cosmic being from Arcturus as he touches our hearts. Gaze into the eyes of the dolphin child as she gazes back at you with great love and reverence. In the company of the flux of dolphins we come back to the shallow waters, and from there we enter into the spiral of light — you and your consort — and we return to the Palace of Shamballa on Venus. The seven Kumaras and the seven consorts offer their blessing to us in the hope that someday we will feel their presence on Earth and that we will see them walking alongside of us. We bless them, and we are blessed by them by placing our hands on their hearts and receiving their hands on our heart. This blueprint is now sealed with the blessing of the planetary Logos, the Sanat Kumara who came to the rescue of Earth many eons ago.

We spiral in the tunnel of light, through the Throne of the Undifferentiated Source that has formed above our antahkarana, our silver-golden cord. We emerge in the presence of the I AM THAT I AM, which every one of you are, every one of us. Returning to our bodies, we hold the vibration of the mother, father, child as the cosmic blueprint for the new Cosmic Christ Consciousness to be illuminated on Earth for the benefit of the ascension of Mother Earth and awakening of all humankind.

With great pleasure and in great gratitude, I bless each and every one of you and the group entity that you have formed. With great joyful celebration of the light that you are and the light that you shine upon Earth and humankind, in the company of the Seven Mighty Elohim of Creation and their consorts, in the presence of the Seven-Fold Flame of Creation, imbued by the power of the perfected magical presence of the I AM THAT I AM, I am your own mother, Elohim Minerva. Blessings.

Metatron

Metatron is a word derived from the Greek which means "the highest throne." "Meta" means "above" or "beyond". This refers to the Throne of God. The energies of Metatron, who is the most loved and revered cosmic and angelic being closest to God, encircle and illumine the Throne of God. He has the power to withstand the blazing fire of God's light. The other beings (mentioned in this book) who can be at or close to the throne are the Seven Mighty Elohim, Uriel and Melchizedek, the universal logos. Metatron is known as the mouth of God or the right hand of God. He was given the dispensation to directly manifest this entire universe by the command of God. He is therefore responsible for creating all creation by externalizing the light from the heart of God. Uriel brought the light of God to the surface, and with it Metatron penetrated into the darkness of matter. He is responsible for all planets and star systems around the great central sun.

Metatron started out as the guardian angel of outer light. In its great love for God and for all the creation (which is its handiwork), Metatron incarnated on Earth as a human being. Through many lifetimes he achieved enlightenment and was elevated to the higher realms occupying the element of fire and becoming a fiery angel. Through this process of descent and then Ascension from Earth, Metatron spiritized matter and materialized spirit. Spiritizing matter is the descent of spirit into the body of matter. Materializing spirit is the elevation of the dark solid body of matter to illumine the light and manifest the divine spark within itself, freeing itself from density and manifesting the spirit of God as light in the realm of matter. Matter — by its nature and because of its density — holds darkness. Materializing spirit is the process of freeing matter from darkness and bringing it to light.

In his book *Kavir-E-Kimia* (Farsi) which translates to *Desert of Alchemy*, Dr. Karim Zargar writes about Metatron in a lifetime as the prophet Enoch. He was taken up to the heavens and shown the mysteries of those realms. At the end of that earthly life Enoch himself went to Heaven and became an angle of fire with 72 wings (36 pairs). He has since spent time as a heavenly creature or a cosmic being. His wings are so wide and his power so vast that when all the angels of heaven stand on one side of God, he can stand on the opposite side and spread his wings to surpass the wingspan and the might of all the other angels put together.

According to *Angels A to Z* pp. 273-275, Metatron is known as the liberating angel who wrestled with Jacob. He also appeared to Abraham, bringing a lamb to prevent Abraham from sacrificing his son. He rescued the Jews after forty years of wandering in the desert, bringing them to safety when he appeared to Moses on the Mount. He became known to Moses and his followers as El-Shaddai or the Lord of the Mountain. He is the protector of humankind, and anyone who prays to him will have the power of his protection bestowed upon them. He will take the prayers of humankind through 900 levels of cosmos to obtain God's attention. In the same way that God is known by many names, so is Metatron known by many names. By calling upon these names one can receive the grace of Metatron. Apart from the well known names such as Metatron and YHWH (Yahweh), he is also known as Ya-Ho-EL, LAD, So-ra-ya and Yo-fi-EL and El, the one who sits by the Throne of God and records the deeds of humankind. Metatron is also known as the Throne of God. In the book *The Mysteries of Zohar*, he is known as one of the cosmic beings with a celestial voice or ha-di. In Sanskrit, Nada means celestial sound and in Persian, Neda is the word which is revealed by God.

I have been consciously working directly with Metatron since 1994. Over time I have noticed that there are different levels of energy vibration and quality that Metatron shows in various channelings. He has told us that seven levels of his being are channeled through my body. The lowest, or rather the closest to human body of matter, is one where he last incarnated as a king in India a few hundred years ago. The highest is a cosmic being who is too pure to withstand the third-dimensional reality and the body of form but is willing to help humankind by lowering her/his vibration to reach our consciousness and deliver the teachings to us. I call this being the seventh aspect of Metatron. She/he only comes to give discourses regarding planetary grids, ceremonies and initiations, She/he delivers the message and leaves. And would not address mundane earthly questions because She/he is far removed from these levels.

In the course of nearly two decades we have performed many ceremonies around the Earth, and Metatron has been the guiding force to bring light to our Earthly reality. The results of these ceremonies become obvious when you read through the various journeys we have completed over the years and the gifts that Earth and humankind has received from the Masters of Light. These gifts have opened up the higher dimensional realms of reality to humankind. I gratefully acknowledge and appreciate all that Metatron and the Masters of Light have accomplished through us. In the first *Gifts* book, we discussed the Upper Gobi Desert as the etheric home of Shamballa on Earth and the ceremonies performed for return of heaven to Earth. In this book, you will read about the palace of Shamballa, the physical home of Sanat Kumara on Venus. You are invited to go on journeys with the Masters to Venus and bathe in the light in various initiation chambers in the temples of Shamballa. The doors of Shamballa have opened up to humankind, and some day the etheric Shamballa on Earth will also be a place we can visit physically. We will receive the blessings and gifts of eternal fire of love from the physical presence of Sanat Kumara on Earth. The spearhead for all of these events has been Metatron. In *Gifts I* and *Gifts II* books, I have explained Metatron more extensively.

Golden Sphere of Righteousness, Compassion and Grace

Commentary: In this meditation, Lord Metatron offers a golden sphere the size of a dollar coin to be placed over the thymus gland chakra. This is the area known as the cosmic heart. This is our connection with the great cosmic heart of the divine. Into this sphere, which is made of 24-karat liquid gold, he places qualities such as non-judgment, righteousness, compassion, grace, mercy, wisdom, love and understanding. He tells us that this sphere has its own consciousness and is capable of bringing those qualities to our heart from the heart of the divine. He then spins this sphere and expands it to go around our solar system to the heart of our sun. There, the sphere connects with the

Father/Mother energies of our solar system and becomes magnified. He repeats this process three times. Each time magnifying the effect 10 times, 100 times, 1000 times more vibrant and effective by interchanging from our heart to the heart of the great Mother/Father sun energies in order to receive greater positive qualities and to clear pain and negativity.

METATRON, CHANNELED APRIL 3, 2004

Beloved of my own heart, I am Metatron. Take a deep breath with me.

Envision in the space of your heart a golden sphere. This golden sphere is the size of the circle that is created when you place the index finger and the thumb of one hand together to make a circle. Envision that this sphere is made of 24-karat gold. Gold on your Earth is a solid metal, yet I would like you to envision it from the etheric point of view, as fluid. As you let go of the density (caused by pollution) and become lighter, you need the fluidity of the elements — not in their solid form — but in their etheric form. The sphere has the quality of 24-karat solid gold but it is liquid. The sphere is held eight to ten inches away from your thymus gland. I will now tell you about the beneficial qualities of having this little globe positioned etherically on top of your thymus gland, and if you then choose to, you may proceed with this exercise.

The qualities of the consciousness held within this sphere are the qualities of a reality that, right now, the Masters of Wisdom are bringing to Earth. This reality is one where light prevails and therefore the qualities of goodness and righteousness, nonjudgment, compassion, grace, mercy, wisdom, understanding, service, camaraderie, union and

Divine Love are prevalent and prominent. All of these qualities in energetic form are encapsulated inside of this sphere. I am placing this sphere in your thymus gland which is truly the gland that rules over the heart and the mind. (It is called the cosmic heart.)

You see, no one as yet has discovered where the mind resides. And in scriptures through parallel and parable there have been references that the true heart and the true mind reside somewhere in the right side of the physical heart. So, I would say that the general area of the thymus gland is the residence of the etheric heart and mind, the cosmic heart and mind — which are not separate from one another. In other words, although we sometimes say the mind of God and at other times we say the heart of God, this separation is only necessary because with human beings there is that separation. From a divine point of view, the mind and the heart are one, and they operate the same way. The cosmic mind and the cosmic heart are the same entity; there is no duality. It is only in duality where you say either you think with your mind or you feel with your heart. In true essence there is nothing to stop you from doing both. You can think with your mind and feel with your heart all at the same time and apply all of that together. Together without separating the two, without interpreting one as good and the other as bad, without causing one to rule over the other, without forcing the mind to overtake the body, without relying on the heart to make all the decisions.

It is not about one or the other. It is about the union of the two. It is about the union of the male and female — mind being male, heart being female. The coming together of the two brings androgyny. And as a result of becoming androgynous we no longer live in duality. As a result of bringing into balance the male and female polarities — whether it is the coming together of the mind and heart, male and female of the species, positive and negative poles, or any other union of duality — the energy of separation is released and we are brought to wholeness.

Do I have your permission to place this golden sphere in your thymus gland? If you are willing to receive, say, " Yes. "

Envision this golden sphere. It is small, very lovely, round, magical, smooth, cool. Before I bring it into you, I will spin it clockwise, from the left side of your body to the front, to the right side and to the back of your body. As it spins faster and faster, it feels as though the air around it becomes almost liquid to the point where it creates a vacuum. Your heart will pull the sphere into itself. Then it is pulled from the heart upwards into the thymus gland and at that point it sparks out. It always will stay encapsulated. But when it sparks out, it feels as though an explosion has taken place, but all that has happened is a fusion. It explodes without losing its entity or identity.

The emanation is no longer only an inch wide. The emanation is mushrooming in every direction into a larger and larger and larger ball of light until your entire body is in a cocoon of light. And the entire room is in this cocoon of light. And the entire building is in this cocoon of light. And then all of your city is cocooned in this ball of light, and all of your state is cocooned in this ball of light. All the waters are cocooned in this ball of light; all of your country and continent are cocooned in this ball of light; all the globe, all of Mother Earth is cocooned in a ball of light. It emanates out from the globe into the solar system.

Right now within the solar system, the construction of a tube of light has been completed. A structure has been created like a band of light, or a tunnel of light. Inside this circular band of light is the entire planetary system of this solar conglomerate. So the sun and all the planets in the solar system are inside this band. We are now emanating your golden sphere throughout this band of light. Emanations going from Earth in all directions to Venus on one side and to Mars on the other. Then expanding to the next two planets, then the next two and then the next two. Ultimately reaching to the sun from both sides, where this Consciousness originated in the first place. So take a deep breath and absorb this energy.

Imagine the physical body of the sun as both a male and female being. In their hearts the same spark is fused, and from the fusion the emanations are 10 times, 100 times, 1000 times greater. Going back in the opposite direction into the tube of light (from both sides of the sun), planetary system by planetary system, coming back to you. There is another explosion, another implosion, another fusion coming back, 10 times, 100 times, 1000 times greater than the one that we sent out. Breathe that in, and bring that into your body to your thymus gland.

NEXT ROUND: See it again emanating even greater from your own sphere. Going out all around, reaching back out into the sun, magnifying, intensifying 10 times, 100 times, 1000 times emanating back, reaching back to you. Receiving it, fusing with it, letting it explode, letting it implode, extend and expand and go all the way around back inside the tube, reaching back to the sun for the next round.

THIRD ROUND: Fusing, uniting, exploding, imploding, emanating, coming back each time faster, each time more profuse. Coming back into your heart and into your thymus gland. You may actually be feeling pain or pressure from the intensity. Breathe it in, hold it in. Feel it vibrating throughout your body. Pause and take a deep breath to absorb and digest all the energies that have been moving through you.

Do this at least once every twenty-four hours, preferably at night before bedtime. If you do it more than once a day, you'll feel the power of it even more (first in the morning and then at night). To anchor it on behalf of Earth and humanity, I request that you do it once a day. To receive benefits for yourselves, do it as many times a day as you can. If you feel pressure on your chest as a result of doing it, then say, "Whatever is standing in the way of the absorption of the energies of the sphere, I ask that it be transmuted and removed. I ask that my resistance be released so that I may absorb the fullness of these energies."

With great love, I stand at your feet as your own father, Metatron. So it is.

Own Your Divinity Through Commandments and Decrees

Commentary: This reading was given on the eve of the Festival of Diwali, or the Festival of Light, the Indian New Year. This day is celebrated as the victory of light over darkness and the return of Goddess Lakshmi to Earth. Lakshmi (Lak-sh-mi) is the Goddess of Spiritual Attainments and Material Abundance. Her light and glory illuminate every household, shop, street corner and place in India at the eve of the Festival of Diwali. Lord Metatron was very pleased with the spiritual progress of the young man receiving this discourse. From the higher realms Metatron brought the divine template for achievement of the divine purpose for all souls who wish to receive it. The young man was calling from India while he was staying at the ashram (holy retreat) of Karunamayi. Karunamayi is a living saint who carries the energy vibration (or incarnation) of Goddess Saraswati, the Goddess of Knowledge and Wisdom. She travels around the world and gives blessings to souls of all faiths and beliefs who go to see her in multitudes (see www.Karunamayi.org).

This is a great gift that Metatron has bestowed upon all of us in his joy and pleasure with his young chela (student). He has told us that it only takes one soul to serve the light before all can benefit from the outcome. The service and the ensuing benefits become established upon the whole grid of the Earth. We can all share in receiving the original blueprint for our divine purpose. This blueprint is what God intended for our divine souls at the beginning of time, before duality and separation made us forget our divinity. By moving away from our divine purpose we lost our divinity, gave up living in bliss of oneness with God, and developed our so-called free will. God in his/her love for us accepts our forgetfulness and allows us to go about roaming the universe doing as we please until such time that we are ready to return to our divine purpose. Then God would willingly accept us to return to oneness.

Oneness can only be achieved when we receive and accept the original template or original blueprint for our divine purpose. As we walk on the path of enlightenment and remember our soul, we can return to the original blueprint and divine plan. To accelerate this process, Metatron has interceded on our behalf because of his pleasure with this one young being and in honor of the event; the Festival of Light or Diwali. We can reap the benefits by receiving this meditation and repeating the exercises to fully embody our divine purpose. Read the following with love and reverence with pure heart, and ask in the name of the I AM THAT I AM that your original divine purpose be restored to you. The more often you repeat this exercise, the sooner you will see results.

Not long ago during a reading, Metatron spoke to my friend Susan and told her that he wanted her to demand and command more from him and from the universe. Her son Ben, listening intently to her summary of the reading afterwards, snatched this nugget of wisdom and put it to use. A few months later, Susan and I arrived in India for the Equinox ceremonies. At our first reading with Metatron, he told Susan that Ben would have a great window of opportunity opening in his life around the first of May, which would extend for a three-year period and would set the pace for the rest of his life. On April 29, he received notification of his acceptance into a local university. He had completed the prerequisite work, and although the chance of acceptance was low given the numbers of applicants and positions available, he had forged ahead and applied. Intending to complete a double major, the coursework required three years.

After receiving the good news, Susan went to Ben's apartment for the first time since arriving home from India. The first thing she saw when he opened the door was a poster on the wall that he had created. On a background of a scroll with angel wings, a sword on one side and a quill on the other, resembling a contract, Ben had written, "Metatron. Manifest. I command Metatron and all light to see to it that I be accepted into UC Berkeley for fall 2005." While Susan was reading the decree, Ben said, "Well, I commanded, and the universe responded, just like Metatron said!"

As Master Jesus said, "For truly I say to you, if you have faith as a mustard seed, you shall say to this mountain, 'Move from here to there,' and it shall move; and nothing shall be impossible to you." (Matthew 17:20). Thank goodness for the purity of heart and the childlike innocence with which this young man heard and heeded in surrender the great voice of wisdom. He chose to change his life to bring his dream into reality. The timeframe that Metatron had given us the news of Ben's three year window of opportunity corresponded to the same time that Ben had put that poster on his wall.

Let us take a deep breath. And we offer this healing for all Earth and all humankind. And may Goddess Lakshmi bestow us with spiritual and material abundance on this auspicious day. And we offer all that we receive in service to light and for the healing of others. May the wisdom of Goddess Saraswati fill our hearts and our minds and bring us to the fulfillment of our divine purpose. May we receive the blessings of Karunamayi. So it is.

METATRON, CHANNELED OCTOBER 12, 2003

Beloved of my own heart, I am Metatron. Take a deep breath with me.

I will talk with you regarding commandments and decrees. It is of utmost importance that you move to the energies of commandments and decrees. The difference between a prayer of supplication and a prayer of commandment and decree is this: in the prayer of supplication you are making yourself helpless and powerless, you are asking, begging and relegating the power to someone else. Even though that someone else may be your own older sister or brother in light (e.g. the Masters), you are relegating your power to them asking them to do things on your behalf. In a prayer of commandment and decree, you admit to your own divinity. You call upon the divine spark of God within you, and by the power of that divine spark you call upon the energies of light to come to your service or to the service of humanity. Through the prayers of invocation, decrees, commands and demands from the Universe, that which is your divine right will be given to you, no questions asked. It is your divine right to be a spark of God; it is your divine right to shine that spark of God upon this Universe.

Please understand the importance of owning your own divinity; standing by the spark of God within you and allowing your own sisters and brothers in light — Ascended Masters — to rub shoulders with you. Don't go down in supplication; don't fall down behind them. **Stand up, stand tall, stand proud, stand by their side, not even a step behind them. Stand by their side. By the mere fact that**

you are in physical incarnation, you have earned the merit to demand and command the Universe to serve you: Demand it, command it, make it happen.

This does not mean be arrogant. **This means the ulti-mate humbleness. Humble yourself to take responsibility for the divinity that is within you. Humble yourself to know that Mastery is awaiting you. Humble yourself to know that your brothers and sisters amongst Ascended Masters are awaiting you, awaiting your divine spark to illuminate your entire Being, so that you can walk amongst them.** Expect and watch them come to sweep you off your feet to their retreats to teach you all that you need to learn. All that you need to learn you already know; all they will do is to bring you to the remembrance of it. They reactivate scientifically at cell structure your memory banks to enable you to recall your divinity.

For them to administer this to you, you must stand in your divine power. This is where your "Divine Will" comes in. This is where you choose. You can choose to be in power and command your divine will or you can continue your prayers of supplication, your prayers of helplessness and hope-lessness. You can choose to remain focused on all the nega-tivity that is ongoing: the greed, the avarice, the pain and the suffering in the world. You can beat your chests till blood comes out with the disharmony in this world, or you can stand tall and claim your divinity. Ask that your divine right be given to you, not tomorrow, but now in this moment. And that it be given to you in all its fulfilling motions, fulfilling you mentally, emotionally, physically and spiritually.

Give up your depression and know that you are depressed on behalf of the world and that this will be lifted up. And the moment that it lifts, you will see the light. Give up your hopelessness and become hopeful, and allow yourself in your own free will to be used as the masters that you are. Let your sisters and brothers amongst the Ascended Masters, the Masters of Wisdom, give you your mastery by preparing your bodies, your minds, your emotions and your spirit. When you are ready, your Ascension, your Mastery, your wisdom, your light and furthermore your divinity is awaiting you.

The doors of the realms of heavenly abodes — the Brotherhoods and the Sisterhoods of the White Lodge — the etheric retreats and Shamballa are opening up to Earth. This will be the final phase of the attainment of the energies. This time period will prepare you to go into the ascension of Earth. The Masters and Mistresses of light will give you an introduction to the field of the Shamballa energies to work with. This will be phase one of the anchoring of the Shamballa energies physically upon Earth. This is the time for great celebration. Know that it is coming.

For many years I have been speaking to you that the year 2005 will be the culmination of all light, that the year 2005 will be the year where all the heavenly gates will be opened up to Earth. I am pleased to tell you that in this period of time, Earth will go into anchoring Shamballa energies, the master energies of the White Lodge, anchoring the energies of the Pure White Light. This is beyond the Seven Rays. The Seven Rays are the product of our separation from the Pure White Light of God force. This is simply the Seven Rays moving in reverse order through the prism and coming out on the other end as Pure White Light. This is the anchoring of

142

the Pure White Light. You will be embodying the energies as the beacons of Pure White Light. You will be transmitting the energies as the antenna. You will be the absorbing forces as well as the transmitting forces; you will become sponges that can hold large quantities of this Pure White Light. As you transmit it, the supply is constantly and continuously replenished within you. In this time you will all learn how to receive the energies of Pure White Light how to transmit the energies of Pure White Light and how to replenish yourselves.

So far you have done a great job of receiving, anchoring and transmitting energies. However, in the process you have drained yourselves. You need to learn to replenish yourself as you transmit it. Continue to be the sponge, absorb as much as possible from the ethers and yet not deprive yourself, anyone, anything or any place. From the transmission of the energies you become a catalyst.

Energy Harmonics from Orion to Achieve Critical Mass

Then there will be the next level of the transmission of the energies of pure white light. The energies of the Kumaras from the Venusian counterpart as well as the energies of the wise sister planet in constellation Orion will fully open up. On August 12, 2002 you had an opening of the energies of Orion for an introductory period of time. In that timeframe a war was waged in the heavens by the intruding factors upon the planetary forces of light. In that war the forces of light won, and the energies of the sister planet Orion opened up to bring greater balance of light and its maintenance to Earth. They will continue to recalibrate the energies of Earth and the Solar System to receive and absorb greater light.

The nature of the light that was transmitted has shifted: the light is now vibrating different frequencies, bringing changes in the harmonic, the notes, the half-tones, the tones, and the octaves of reality on Earth. This I say for those of you who understand these matters. It is not necessary to become mentally engaged in any of this. Suffice it to say that the Orion energies change the attunement of Earth to ignite the divine spark and to best serve the pure white light. That formula has been found. As of January 19, 2005, those energies are pouring to Earth fast and furiously, from Orion through Venus. In Shamballa on Venus these energies become digestible, absorbable and understandable by planet Earth. This will assist the process of full Ascension for Mother Earth and full awakening of humanity to their divinity. (Ascension of Mother Earth does not mean death of anyone or anything. It means moving to higher vibration of light, clearing and cleansing of Earth and release of mental and emotional dross.)

Those awakened souls, those in various levels of initiation will reach levels of Mastery among the unconscious unawakened human population, multitudes and masses will gain their wakefulness and take the first level of initiation. By August 12, 2005, you achieve critical mass. Critical mass relates to the entry of the 1000 years of peace upon the planet. We enter the reign of peace at March Equinox of 2005, and the energies of truth, mercy, compassion, purity and innocence are restored to Earth. While this is going on upon your planet, it is your job to be the masters and the light beacons that you are meant to be. And know that in the heavens above, who you are, what you are and what you do for your own soul growth and in service to humanity and Mother Earth is greatly appreciated.

In the presence of the hierarchies of the Ascended Masters, Masters and Mistresses of Wisdom, the Brotherhoods and the Sisterhoods of the White Lodge, in the Assembly of the Elders around the Throne of God, in the Assembly of the Karmic Boards, I bid you love, I bid you light, I bid you pure white light from my own heart. I am your father and your humble servant Metatron. And so it is.

(Note: This discourse was given by Lord Metatron on December 12, 2003. It is now April of 2005, and I have just returned from India completing the March equinox ceremonies for the entry of the energies of the 1000 years of peace and truth. If you look at my website (www.NasrinSafai.com) today (April 10, 2005), you will find a range of discourses given by Masters Metatron, Hilarion, Mother Mary, and Quan Yin on the energies of peace, truth, mercy, compassion, purity and innocence. What utterly amazes and humbles me is that I have neither planned nor even remembered that Lord Metatron gave us the above discourse and that the Masters have been bringing these energies in that exact order stated above from November of 2004 until now. Blessed be the light that shines upon us so brightly. May we feel the love and know the order that resides in those higher powers who guide us — that same power that Metatron urges us to own and express in our individual lives.)

Receiving the Original Template and Blueprint For Your Divine Purpose

Commentary: Metatron calls from the heartcore of the Undifferentiated Source the original blueprint and the template for your divine purpose. The divine purpose is what the spirit of God within each of us would plan as our divine mission, for each lifetime and throughout all lifetimes of our soul's journey in embodiment. In this exercise the blueprint for the divine mission — purpose — is installed inside all of your chakras beginning from the top of your head. On top of your head in the crown chakra resides a lotus with one thousand petals. It is believed that as a human being attains heights of spiritual wisdom, the petals of the lotus open up more and more until in full blossom. Through the lotus of the crown, Metatron invites first the energies of the I AM Presence, and then he brings the original divine blueprint and the divine template. He then moves down through every chakra, establishing the template and blueprint in the body. He then calls the highest contract of service for each person. This new contract, if you wish to receive it, will help to move you to greater acts of service to the light and to the masters of light and wisdom.

METATRON, CHANNELED NOVEMBER 11, 2004

Beloved of my own heart, I am Metatron. Take a deep breath with me.

CROWN CHAKRA: The Presence of the I AM THAT I AM will come forward in a silhouette of an enlightened, illumined being of light. As the Presence of the I AM is being received by the crown chakra, I call forth the original perfected blueprint and the original template for the divine purpose of our beloved *(say your name)*. The original perfected blueprint and the original divine template for the divine purpose throughout the entire soul lineage is called for. I ask for the downloading of the template and the blueprint in the crown chakra. As the Presence of the I AM THAT I AM lodges itself in this chakra, I, Metatron, ask also that energies of the divine template and the original blueprint to be downloaded in the crown chakra. *Say: "In the name of the I AM THAT I AM through the intercession of Lord Metatron, I* now ask for the downloading of the divine template and the original blueprint to be completed in the crown chakra."

THIRD EYE CHAKRA: As we move the energies from the crown chakra inside of the head, immersing the third eye in the energies of the I AM THAT I AM, the downloading of the divine template and the original blueprint will be completed in the area of the third eye. *Say: "In the name of the I AM THAT I AM and through the intercession of Lord Metatron, I now ask for the downloading of the divine template and the original blueprint to be completed in the area of the third eye."*

THROAT CHAKRA: We move down the energies into the entire space of the head cavity and we bring it forth to the throat chakra. The original divine template and the original perfected blueprint are downloaded into the area of the crown chakra, the third eye, and now the throat. The throat. A blue light is emanating from the throat chakra. A nile blue light. The nile blue light is the color of the perfected original blueprint. This nile blue is now holding within it the codes; the codes for the template of the divine purpose and the codes for the original perfected blueprint. *Say: "In the name of the I AM THAT I AM and through the intercession of Lord Metatron, I ask for and receive the nile blue codes for the template of divine purpose and the original perfected blueprint in the throat chakra."*

HEART CHAKRA: From the crown chakra to the third eye to the throat chakra, this blue color is moving and merging, moving down the throat, into the arms, the shoulders, the hands. From the neck to the arms, the shoulders, the hands; you may feel a tingling sensation in the hands. As it moves down the chest cavity, the thymus gland, the cosmic heart, as it moves further down filling the lungs, filling the spinal column, moving down from the thymus gland which is the cosmic heart, to the personal heart. The physical muscle and organ we know as the physical heart and the physical heart chakra which sits at the center of the chest. And the physical organs of the lungs, moving down, midnight blue. The original perfected blueprint and the original divine template which holds the divine purpose for *(say your name)* is now being downloaded. And I ask that you take a deep breath and that you find the spinning of the wheel or the chakra in the center of your heart, center of your heart chakra in the middle of your chest. And sit with this energy for a moment. *Say: "In the name of the I AM THAT I AM and through the intercession of Lord Metatron, I now ask for and receive the downloading of the original perfected blueprint and the original divine template for the divine purpose for the cosmic heart, personal heart, lungs, thymus gland, organs, muscles, tissues and veins."*

SOLAR PLEXUS CHAKRA: And now I move the energy again, the original divine template and the original perfected blueprint, to the area of solar plexus. And as I spin it, I want you to envision that all the disempowerment and all the fears and all that you have held onto which no longer serves you is now being released. Your power center is now filled with the downloading of all the codes of your original divine template and with your original perfected blueprint for the divine purpose for which you have come to this earth from the very beginning of time. And all the energies that have created obstacles for you, obstacles on the path of your power, on the path of you holding your power in your hands and offering it to your divine purpose; all these obstacles are now removed. Just as all returns to its source, whether it is light or darkness, here and now, all returns to its source to make way and room for the return of the purity and innocence in the space of the solar plexus. *Say: "In the name of the I AM THAT I AM and through the intercession of Lord Metatron, I now ask for and receive the downloading of the original template and original blueprint for my divine purpose to be downloaded to my solar plexus. This will purify my power center and bring me to the state of purity and innocence as intended in the original blueprint for my divine purpose."* A midnight blue vibration is emanating. The codes are downloading. The original intention for the divine power is restored. The original seat of the soul is cleared and cleansed. The solar plexus is the seat of the soul. The soul resides in the lotus of the solar plexus. There is a large lotus opening in the solar plexus, and the soul is now given a chance to blossom and bloom and to come to its fullness by realizing its true identity and by re-encoding its divine purpose. The recalibration of the solar plexus brings with it the memories of the divine purpose for which you have incarnated on Earth. As I spin this wheel, all the dross and pain, fears and suffering, grief and sorrow is now transmuted and turned into light. What remains is the power to live life according to the divine purpose, divine truth and the divine will of God. God's will be done. God's will be done. God's will be done. In the name of the I AM THAT I AM, God's will be done. In the name of the I AM THAT I AM, God's will be done. In the name of the I AM THAT I AM. You may find yourself slightly nauseous as a result of the spinning of this wheel.

Take deep breaths as I move the energy into a faster spin in the area of your solar plexus. Envision the energy spinning in your belly faster and faster, emanating deep blue light.

SACRAL PLEXUS CHAKRA: I now move the energy down from the solar plexus to the sacral plexus. The original divine template, the original divine blueprint in the Presence of the I AM THAT I AM is now downloaded in all the reproductive organs. Midnight blue is emanating in every which direction as I begin to spin this chakra, releasing all the dross, pain and suffering from many lifetimes, bringing the original state of purity and innocence. *Say: "In the name of the I AM THAT I AM and through the intercession of Lord Metatron, I now ask and receive the downloading of the original blueprint for the sacral plexus and reproductive organs."*

ROOT CHAKRA: As I move down the energy of the original divine template — the original perfected blueprint — to the area of the root chakra, midnight blue begins to spin in the root chakra. Energy emanates into the hips, down the legs moving from the thighs to the calves to the ankles and to the feet. Then moving from the bottom of the feet into the core crystal of Mother Earth. The original divine blueprint emanating into the core crystal of Mother Earth. As I spin this wheel in the root chakra, you will find yourself more grounded and connected to the energies of Mother Earth. Your own divine purpose from the realms above is now connected to the Earth below. As above, so below. As below, so above. As within, so without. As without, so within. *Say: "In the name of the I AM THAT I AM and through the intercession of Lord Metatron, I now ask and receive the downloading of the original blueprint for my divine purpose in my root chakra, in my legs connecting me to Mother Earth, bringing me groundedness and great abundance from the resources of our Mother Earth.* " Take a deep breath with me as I spin this wheel, recalibrating the root chakra. Now take a deep breath with me.

This energy field will continue to emanate in your body for a period of seven days. The downloading of the blueprint and the divine purpose and the original template will continue to decode every strand of your DNA. Ultimately, you will find yourself reconnecting with your original soul purpose, and you will find yourself in much closer intimate communion with the heartcore of your own soul and the lineage from which you have come. In this auspicious moment while receiving the template and the blueprint, state your intentions, your wishes or desires for personal or global purposes. Know that whatever you ask for has already been answered and received in this realm of reality by the grace of the I AM THAT I AM, if it is for your highest good.

In the name of the I Am that I Am, it is so.

(Author's Note: Take a deep breath as you state your personal and global intentions, and sit in meditation for a while absorbing these energies. Take three deep breaths when you are ready to come out of meditation, and feel your energy fully return into your body.)

Receiving a New Contract for Highest Service to The Light

From the point of light within the mind of God, I call forth the Threads of Light. I call forth the Threads of Light. I call forth the Threads of Light. In the essence of the Threads

151

of Light, I wrap you from the top of your head to the bottom of your feet, in the cocoon of the filaments of bright white light which are Threads of Light connected to the mind of God. Golden white light that come from their source within the mind of God. As I wrap you in this energy field, you are now pulled from this Earthy realm to enter into the realm of the divine presence in the mind of God. As we move into the presence of the mind of God, invoke the highest possible contract that you can perform in this lifetime, from this moment onward. Ask the contract to be downloaded to your physical body, emotional body, mental body, spiritual body, soul, spirit and your essence.

I wrap you in the filament of light. I take you before the presence of the mind of God, and I intercede on your behalf. Ask in your own words, in the presence of the mind of God, that the highest contract of service be given to you to supercede all other contracts. Ask to be moved to that elevation of light where you may be of the greatest service to the Masters of Wisdom, the Ascended Masters and the Brothers and the Sisters of the White Lodge. *Take a deep breath. Pause and ask in your own words what contract of service you wish to receive. Ask, my beloved, and you shall receive. Knock and it shall be opened unto you. So it is.* In the name of the I AM THAT I AM from the mind of God, we ask forth the presence of a new contract, the highest vibrational force field for the divine purpose of *(say your name)*, in the light of the I AM THAT I AM, through the intercession of Metatron and the Brotherhoods and Sisterhoods of the White Lodge.

I, Metatron now intercede on behalf of *(say your name)* for the downloading of the original blueprint for the highest contract of service to light, to supercede all other contracts. This new contract vibrates to the highest and the purest essence of pure white light, and will place *(say your name)* in service of the Brotherhoods and the Sisterhoods of the White Lodge, the Ascended Masters of Light, and the Masters of Wisdom. **May the service to the Masters of Wisdom bring the light of leadership in purity and innocence to the Planet. May the light of the purity and innocence supercede all lower vibrations. May the return of the original blueprint be downloaded in the bodies, souls, minds and spirits of every being, every consciousness of every essence, of all people, places and things, as well as in the bodies of sentient and non-sentient beings and in all the souls in all levels and dimensions of reality of Earth. Above Earth, below Earth, within Earth and around Earth. All souls, all levels, all dimensions, to receive the highest light, to receive the highest purpose. In the name of the I AM THAT I AM.**

I now pause for a moment for the downloading of this new contract into every cell, molecule, iota, atom and every electron of your body and your being. Take a deep breath as the molecular structure is recalibrated to receive the highest contract from the mind of God. Pause, take a deep breath and meditate to absorb and embody the vibrations of light emanating from the Masters. If there are any doubts or concerns, bring all the self-criticism and self-doubt before the Brotherhoods of the White Lodge and ask that they would annihilate it for you. I will also do this through the grace that has been bestowed upon me. I will give you the help to remember and to vanquish self-criticism and self-doubt as an on-going process. It is important that you ask daily for it to be released from your energy body through the help and assistance of Metatron and the Masters for the next 22 days. We also ask through the downloading of the original blueprint and the divine template for all that is of lack and of fear to be replaced by joy, union and pure white light. So it is.

Sanat Kumara Offers Initiation Into Service of The Light

In joy and gratitude of receiving the initiation to the highest contract, I now take you through the gates of the heavenly realms, in the direction of the North. And bring you to the gateway of the Lodge. As we stand in front of the golden gateway, we offer ourselves in the name of the light, in service to the light. We ask that the doors be opened in the name of the I AM THAT I AM. The golden gateway opens up, and I bring you to the Great Hall in the assembly of the Brotherhoods of the White Lodge. Feel the vibration of light emanating from the multitudes of the Masters of Light.

You are taken by two members of the Brotherhood into an inner chamber. Inside, there is a chair. Take your seat upon the chair, and receive your scepter of power. You are bestowed with the crown of glory. A beam of light begins to emanate from above the chair. Stand in the presence of this beam of light. Bathe in pure white light, and see it emanating from every cell of your body. You are being prepared to receive the presence and the essence of Sanat Kumara, the highest member of the Seven Kumaras, who holds the energy vibration of Earth within his own heart. His light sustains the Earth and all Earthly souls. Sanat Kumara places his left hand on your heart, and you place your left hand on his heart. This is a swearing-in ceremony to become a member of the Lodge of the Kumaras. With this, you move into the service of the Kumaras. The range of services are: to rescue the Earth from all darkness and to move it into pure white light, to be in the service of pure white light. You stand shoulder to shoulder with all the Kumaras and all Brotherhoods and the Sisterhoods of the White Lodge for as long as necessary, throughout the eons of time, for this task to be completed. You are now receiving your initiation from the presence of Sanat Kumara. Receive your guidance Receive your initiation. Receive your blessing. Now take a deep breath. If there is a boon (gift) you wish to receive or a desire that you wish to express before the presence of Sanat Kumara and the Masters, express your desire now.

Remember, it is your divine right to come to this place, which is your own home, and to be in the presence of these Masters. It is your divine right to request an audience with them and ask for their presence to be known to you in any given moment, day or night. And it is your divine right to request higher light to shine upon humanity, upon your own beingness and upon the path of light on which you walk. It is your divine right to ask for the intercession of the Masters of Wisdom, the Ascended Masters of Light and the Cosmic Beings of Light. It is your divine right to enter into the mind of God (with permission) — through emanating and vibrating to the Threads of Light that are sent out from the mind of God — to ask the intercession of the highest vibration of light and to request the highest contract. That highest contract, in any given moment of your life, can bring you to the next level and elevation of light.

You have now moved to that level and elevation of light. That light is emanating as you move through each day. When that light comes into contact with the pollution and the density on this mundane level of existence, its vibration may be lowered. For this reason, it is beneficial that you ask frequently for the recalibration of that light. Wrap yourself in the Threads of Light and return to the mind of God again and again to renew the contract, to review the contract, to recalibrate the contract, to serve on the highest vibration of light and to offer the highest possible service. Before we leave the Lodge, if you have any question, statements or desires, express them now. The great beings know everything that goes through your mind. Pause. Take a deep breath. Ask any questions.

So it is. The initiation to the service of the Kumaras in the presence of the Brotherhoods of the White Lodge is now complete. Returning from the chamber, stand in the center of the Great Hall and feel the love and the celebration from every member of the Lodge. Receive this love in your heart, and remember that this is your divine right. The return to this place is a homecoming, and you are always welcome to return. Take a deep breath as we move through the Great Hall. Receive all the joy and love that is pouring out from the Masters, feel it with every cell and vibration of your beings, and know that this is all happening in the celebration of your own glory. You have attained yet another recalibration to the highest vibration of light.

We now bless the presence of every individual member of the Lodge; the Seven Kumaras, the Masters of Wisdom, the Ascended Masters of Light, the Cosmic Beings of Light, the essence of Metatron, the energies of the mind of God.

As we return to the golden gateway, in preparation for the return journey to the heartcore of Mother Earth, we bid gratitude, thanksgiving and love to all the beings of light.

Beloved of my own heart, in the days to come, you will feel the changes in your own heart, mind, body and beingness. This process that we have together established will continue for a 22 day period. In this time, you will move through other levels of initiation physically, as well as mentally, emotionally and etherically, and many changes will happen energetically in your body. Take good care of your physical body, drink a lot of water and beneficial liquids; listen to your body and heed its desires. An energy exchange takes place when you listen to your body. You will know what is beneficial for your body because your body will crave for it. Eat mostly raw fruits and vegetables for the next 22 days to allow a greater absorption of these energies. You may need a lot of sleep; heed that need. The process of receiving the energies takes place during dream time. Allow yourself as much sleep time as possible. Plan to take a nap mid-morning or early afternoon if you can. Make a point of going to bed early at night to give your body time to process these energies. Your body may have different needs and cravings than you are used to during the 22 day period and possibly even afterwards. Remember that all the love and light of the universe is supporting you on your path of divine service.

In that love and light, I am your father, Metatron. So it is.

Venus, Home of Shamballa: Journey Through the Portal of Light

Commentary: This discourse was given the day before the full alignment of the Harmonic Concordance of November 8, 2003. We received this meditation when the alignment of six major planetary bodies made a perfect six-pointed star and amidst solar and lunar eclipses and major solar flares. A lunar eclipse was in progress as this discourse was given. There were many solar flares, and many people were down energetically, sleepless and exhausted.

Lord Metatron brought the feminine life force energies from the palace of Shamballa on Venus to heal our tired and weary bodies, which were bombarded with the fire of transmutation from solar flares and Harmonic Concordance. He then took us on a journey to Orionis in the Constellation Orion in the company of the Great Being from Venus to receive the masculine life force energies of the Orion for the balancing of our body and beingness. After the release that came from the events of Concordance, he filled us with the new mother/father energies to help us heal and renew our beingness.

Lord Metatron also speaks of synchronic lines in these journeys. These are interplanetary highway systems where information and light travels. Synchronic lines are therefore gateways for the alignments of events and information. Inside of these tunnels of light, thoughts can become manifest with greater speed and forcefulness. If there is a place where the adage "thoughts are things" would be true, it would be inside the synchronic lines.

Beloved of my own heart, I am Metatron. Take a deep breath with me.

Envision in front of you a portal of light. It is in the shape of a diamond. The size of this portal is about ten inches from top to bottom and about eight inches from left to right, point to point. This portal is positioned approximately twelve inches outside of your heart chakra suspended in air. In other words, if you draw a line from the center of your chest outward to a distance of one foot and then look down at your chest, you will see this portal of light. This portal has its own consciousness. In the center, there is a vertical eye. It is a slit in the very center that looks like an eye. The eye is pointed north to south, and the pupil of the eye is looking down in the direction of South. The central point of the eye is very important because when that portal opens, I want to take you on a journey.

Inside the diamond, between where that eye sits and the four edges of the portal, you'll notice translucent emerald green fluid light. These are new energies that we are bringing through, and your bodies are sensitive to these energies. Focus your attention on that emerald green fluid light. I would like to call upon the Great Being from Venus to take you on this journey. This is a being of light whose name I shall not give you. I will simply use the name of the Great Being from Venus. Someday as you get more and more involved with these energies, you will get to know this being better. Once you know the essence of this being, you will open up to newer higher vibrations of light. For now, the Great Being from Venus will suffice. Your consciousness must move to the eye, and when you arrive at the other side you will be in a time warp, and through the time warp you will be taken through a tunnel of time space continuum which opens up to you. At the very end of that tunnel the Great Being is waiting for you.

Our first point of entry is planet Venus itself. You are suspended in the air and observing the vibration of this planet as we approach it. The great system of the planet vibrates an emerald green and purple light. Shimmering, shining, golden purple and emerald green light. There is a great deal of activity going on around the great system of this planet.

If you turn around and look at the Earth from space, you would see that she is imbued by a ball of orange-red light. This is what is happening at this present moment to your planet. She is burning the dross, and every one of you is burning your dross. All the negativity is coming to the surface. You are experiencing it in the form of hardship and negative things that may be happening in your lives. These hardships have a wide range: someone you trust is taking advantage of you, your own child is acting strangely, people that you have called coworkers are betraying you, you are losing the job that you trusted for so long, people you have worked with don't deserve or desire your friend-ship because they are showing their true colors, people around you are acting selfishly, people are choosing con-frontations rather than compassionate solutions. All of this is the burning of the dross.

To ultimately choose compassionate solutions, human beings have to burn their conflictive behavior. To burn the conflictive behavior, they have to bring it to the surface. To bring it to the surface, they have to act on it. And that applies in a large spectrum from border to border, point to point for people, places and things. It is not just happening in one area. As you can see, the entire planet is imbued by the fire of conflict. The solar flares are not affecting one location differently from others. They are affecting all, everywhere. The entire globe, your planet, is immersed in these energies. It is also important to understand that these energies will go on to become accelerated as they continue on this path. As they burn, they turn into light. And in order to burn, the sun of your own solar system helps you by sending more fire to your atmosphere in the form of the solar flares.

We approach the atmosphere of planet Venus. You are now in the presence of the Great Being. As you begin to descend in the atmosphere or the auric field of Venus, you feel a new sense of peace and calmness. We are entering through the synchronic lines which look like a tunnel of golden light. From a distance it may look like you are entering into filaments of gold, liquid light. It is actually a tunnel of liquid light when you enter it. As you glide through it, you turn into liquid matter yourself (the body is not as solid as it is on Earth).

A golden gateway begins to open up as you approach with the Great Being, and as you enter into the great hall notice that everything around you has a golden-pink hue. This is the Great Hall in the Palace of Shamballa. In the center of that hall, there is an oval shaped stage that is set much like a very large altar. You may step on the first tier of this raised stage. As you stand on the first step, you have a greater view and better feel for what is on the altar. As you stand in that position, say a prayer and make a wish. The Great Being will take his/her position in the very center of that stage, and an illumination of light begins to vibrate like a pillar that extends outwards emanating toward you, entering through your heart chakra, your third eye and your solar plexus. This feels like liquid gold. Pause for a long moment and breathe deeply, absorbing all the light and feminine vibration that you are receiving. Take a few long breaths. Absorb the light and intend it to stay with you.

The emanations of light recede. The Great Being steps down, and you are beckoned to leave in the same way that you entered. As you move to the golden gateway, let us bless this opportunity to receive such high illumination of light from the Palace of Shamballa. Take a deep breath and pause to receive the full effect of these energies.

(Note: Continue this meditation with the following discourse as Lord Metatron takes us to the planet Orionis in the center of constellation Orion in the company of the Great Being of Venus.)

Journey to Orion for Light and Compassion

Commentary: Although the five days of Harmonic Concordance have passed, we can always connect with the energies and request the clearing that we need to be provided to us, wherever in the scheme of things we may be. Remember, time as we know it, does not exist. All things are happening simultaneously in space. Time and space are one and the same continuum except from our linear point of view. In our duality we see them as separate entities. When the Masters tell us that we can create our own reality, they are asking us to pick and choose from the events that are sitting inside the time-space continuum according to the universal law of Divine Love, in harmony, peace and compassion. Not because of some cause we created at 5 a.m., which invokes a reaction by 6 a.m., which then needs to be rectified the following day, the following year, or even the following lifetime!

This journey should follow after the journey to Venus in the previous chapter. The previous chapter was about receiving the feminine principle. This journey is about receiving the masculine principle.

METATRON, CHANNELED NOVEMBER 7, 2003

Beloved of my own heart, I am Metatron. Take a deep breath with me.

We move through the golden gateway entering into the tunnel of light, in the presence of the Great Being. We shall proceed to planet Orionis in the constellation Orion. Entering through the time-space continuum in the tunnel of light, accelerating faster and faster until everything becomes a point of light. Then you begin to slow down and see the atmosphere of Orionis, a planet in the center of the constellation Orion.

This planet has a very different energy. An energy which feels as though liquid gold was poured around it. There are no other colors but liquid gold. This planet is very strong, very powerful, very wise, very masculine. Whereas Venus, with all the purples and all the greens and the liquid lights — the shimmering lights with energy emanating around it — is an expanded state of the Feminine Principle, this one is the concentrated form of the Masculine Principle. This is

163

why it is important for the combined energies of Orion and Venus to create a double Helix — the Mother and Father — aligning with one another so that the Earth can be the child, creating the triune aspect. Orion as the Father, Venus as the Mother. Earth as the child. With the sun of your solar system as the Godfather and the Moon as the Godmother.

As you become immersed in the energy of the atmosphere of Orion, all you see is liquid gold. It will take you a moment to acquaint yourself with these energies and realize that you are also entering into the synchronic line, yet another time tunnel. You are entering through the golden gateway into the Great Hall where the energy is very grand and extremely strong. The energy is very anchored, very focused. The energy is like a laser beam, compared to Venus where the energy emanates and expands. This is a laser beam fully focused. Very different from anything you experience on Earth because of its strength and its grand nature. It automatically requires your respect and your reverence. It automatically brings you to your knees as though you are standing in the Presence of the Holy Father.

Here also, in the center there is a golden oval shaped altar with a raised stage. In the middle around the edge of the stage is a platform. As you step onto the platform you get a better view of the top of the stage. The Great Being will take his/her position in the center. The pillar of light descends. The emanations move through the Great Being and enter your crown chakra, your thymus and your personal heart. Pause, take a deep breath and absorb the energies. Close your eyes. Take a few deep and long breaths.

We will exit in the same way that we entered. You will move through the golden gateway, into the time-space continuum, through the tunnel of light. You are speeding to the point of light, through the point of light back into your own solar system and into the atmosphere of Earth. And again, as you come in, notice the fire; the orange colored light that is emanating from Earth. I bring you back to your bodies and I ask you to hold on to these energies and practice these meditations for seven days from today. It is very important that you focus your energies on building a future of light, love and compassion during the seven day period. Realize that what you will put into your personal grid for this time, will impact the next seven years. Be positive, be vigilant, be clear.

And write down your thoughts. The moment you begin writing down your thoughts, you will process them — right there — and then something new will emerge from those thoughts that you would not have noticed if you do not give yourself time to write them down. Make a ceremony and a prayer for light and for compassion out of everything that you do: the food that you eat, the clothes that you put in the wash, the thoughts that come to your mind, the drive in the car, the cleaning that you do.

Cleaning (your home, car, office and your body) is very important right now. As you clean and relieve yourself of all that no longer serves you, symbolically you are cleansing your own emotional and mental bodies and releasing the dirt from your own body and being. Release all those things that no longer serve you. Go through mental processes, sift through thoughts, realize that certain thoughtforms which have brought you certain realities no longer serve you.

Then release those that have no place in your future and give them up to this ball of light, this ball of fire that your planet is in right now. Your planet has become "yagna," a fire pit for sacred ceremonies for the span of the five days of Harmonic Concordance 2003. This is the best time to burn or transmute anything you don't want. Transmute the unhappiness, transmute the sadness, burn the pain of the energy of people who have abused you, situations where you have felt mistreated, those you have misbehaved towards, and those who have misbehaved in your direction. People, places and things need to be cleared and cleansed of their dross to bring them to the state of purity and innocence that was originally intended in the Divine Plan. The purpose of these five days of burning is to clear the multitudes and masses and the consciousness of all souls from all impurities and to reinstate the state of purity and innocence.

I bring you back to the portal. Move through the golden gateways through the diamond-shaped portal and begin to see the emerald green. The eye will open up for you to move through. Once on this side you simply lodge yourselves back in your bodies and I close the portal.

With great love, and the joy of being in your presence, I am your Father Metatron.

Thoth

Introduction

As Ascended Master Thoth, this being has been involved with the evolution of Earth for more than 30,000 years. Perhaps one of the longest standing Ascended beings, he has been known as one of the gods by more than one faith on Earth throughout time. In the time of Egypt he was Tahuti, the God of Justice, who wore the Ibis bird headdress. As the Atlantean God his name was Chikutet. In the Emerald Tablets he declares that anyone who wishes to commune with him must call him three times by his name Chikutet Arlich Vemilitus. As the Mayan God he appears as the serpent plumed Quetzalcoactl (Ketz-Al-Co-Atel). As the God of the Incas, he is Viracoha. As the Persian Messenger of God, Zarathustra (Za-ra-toos-tra) or Zoroaster (Zo-Ra-Ster). As the God of the Greeks, he is Hermes and Hermes Trismejistus, that is Three Times Glorified because he seems to have incarnated and resurrected three times. As Mercury, he is the God of the Romans. He returned back to Earth after his service in the heavens as Mercury to bring to the Earthlings the secret mysteries of the lesser gods' plot against humankind.

As Tehuti or Tehuty he is known as the wisest of the Egyptian gods. He wears the mask of the Ibis bird, which is a fish-eating bird that lived in the reeds grown along the Nile River during the time of the majesty of Egypt. He is usually depicted with the head of an Ibis as his headdress and holds a scroll in his hand. In the scroll is written the mysteries of all creation. He is the keeper of all the records of humankind's evolution on Earth. He is therefore the knower of the Akasha and the keeper of the Akashic records. These records are the account of every soul's deeds on Earth throughout multitudes of incarnations. When he brought the mysteries from Atlantis to Egypt he had to create languages for human beings to communicate with one another, as humanity had fallen to levels of darkness where the knowledge of communication through telepathy was closed. Thoth created all five sacred languages which are the roots of all spoken word on the planet.

The greatest magician, Tahuti knew all the secrets of all realities as he was appointed by the Sun God "Ra" to create those realities. Knower of the secrets of light and dark, in the Emerald Tablets he gives many of the secrets of conquering for the light and bypassing or rather remaining unharmed by the dark lords. The Emerald Tablets are fourteen pallets of imperishable materials upon which he wrote the secret mysteries of the universe and the means to become invincible to the dark. These tablets were to be discovered by people he had appointed in secret crypts somewhere in South America at a predetermined time. The tablets have been translated with a commentary by Doreal in *The Emerald Tablets of Thoth the Atlantean*.

As the Atlantean priest, he is believed to have built the great Temples of Wisdom and Knowledge in Atlantis and have imparted the knowledge directly to priests and priestesses of the temples. As the record keeper of all civilizations, he knows the deeds of all souls. As the caretaker of the Atlantean civilization, he brought all the wisdom and knowledge to Egypt and is known by many names such as Tehuti, Zehuti, Sheps and the Lord of the Khemenu. Egypt was known as the land of Khem and Egyptians as the

Khemenu. The knowledge of alchemy which means "from Chem (Khem)" is the secret of turning base metal into gold. Thoth brought these mysteries from Atlantis to Khem (Egypt). He anchored the knowledge in different parts of the world to prevent the loss of the secret mysteries as a result of the demise of one civilization. He brought the same mysteries to the land of the Mayans and became known as Quetaelcoatl.

To the Greeks, he was known as Hermes and Hermes Trismegistus because he had appeared and disappeared in the history of the Greek empire in three different eras. He is believed to have appeared as the prophet Zarathustra or Zoroaster during the great days of the Persian empire. During this time, the people of the land of Persia were of Zorastrian faith, revering the glory of the sun and respecting the element of fire by keeping it upon sacred altars in every home and temple. To the Romans of the Roman empire, he was known as the God Mercury who knew the secrets of astrology and cosmology and brought those secrets to Earth to help the Earthlings (human beings) overcome the curse of the lesser gods who were jealous of God's love for humanity.

As Hermes he brought forth the great body of material known as *Hermetica*. This is the story of the creation of humankind by the God of all Gods and the resistance of the lesser gods to accept humanity as having equal rights and value as them. Hermes recounts the attempt by the lesser gods of heavens and Earth to convince the God of Gods to allow them to test humankind by throwing the obstacles of the signs of zodiac on the path of their growth. God of all Gods agreed to this test, and the twelve Gods of the zodiac went to work on this project. Jupiter, Mars, Neptune, Mercury, Pluto and other lesser gods developed the astrological influences that affect each human from the moment of birth and throughout each lifetime. As the planets move through the different astrological signs, they leave marks and traits that become positive or negative influences in the lives of those humans beings.

In the teachings of *Hermetica*, Hermes brought from the heavenly realms the secret mysteries to overcome those obstacles. As Mercury, Hermes himself was one of those lesser gods. Therefore he had access to the secrets of the gods. The materials and the body of knowledge that became *Hermetica* also gives the secrets of alchemy, the art of turning base metal into gold, literally and metaphorically as well as spiritually. I do apprise you however, that reading this material is one thing, but understanding and applying it is quite another matter. For more information, read *The Hermetica: The Lost Wisdom of the Pharaohs* by Timothy Freke and Peter Gandy. When you understand the concepts and put them to work, you have obviously earned the merit to turn base metal into gold, overcome the influences of zodiac and all the negative traits of your birth signs and quite possibly attain enlightenment. As hard a read as it may be, we are grateful for the attempts that Master Thoth made in his lifetime as Hermes and as the God Mercury.

When you call upon the presence of Master Thoth and other great and powerful Masters of light, please remember to say something like this: *"The electromagnetic influence of the light and energy of the Masters will not affect the electromagnetic charge of my house, shop, space, car, room (name whatever space you are using)."* Master Thoth is especially powerful in moving electrical currents of energy through whatever medium he is using. Our bodies are perfectly capable of receiving and digesting these energies, and our angels and elemental devas who are in charge of our protection go to work diligently. The electrical equipment however, is a different story. I always take an extended warranty for my recording equipment. On average a decent quality recorder that is used daily would last me a few months, but if used consistently for Master Thoth it may last no longer than four or five channeling sessions. A couple of recorders ran through only one session and refused to work ever again. Usually I have more than one recording system going because invariably, the magnetic strip of the cassette tapes can't handle the charge. The tapes come out with my voice announcing the date and name of the workshop, the participants say their name out loud, and the rest is silence with static.

In our first *Hermetica* workshop series at Women of Wisdom in Easton, Massachusetts, we came out of the session to be informed that all the electrical equipment was burned out. My dear friend Katie, the owner, was extremely graceful about the whole matter and took it at her stride. Master Thoth had come full of power and zest for his first appearance here and none of the tapes had recorded anything either. I did remember to say the protection invocation from then on. Nothing went wrong with the electricals but the recordings remained sporadic. Some sessions were taped and others were not. I do believe that the energies which were not to be repeated simply did not record and all the rest did.

A session at a friend's house was a different story however. I had been instructed by the Masters to invoke and to bring the energies of Master Jesus and Christ Maitreya for the group to experience. The following day after the session, my friend discovered that the electrical equipment and wiring were not working in that entire zone in her house where we had invoked the Masters — upstairs and downstairs, including the automatic electrical switches and the television sets. The electrician informed her that all her wires had burned to a crisp. She also was very graceful about the whole matter but brought it up in one of her readings with Master Jesus. She asked why such a large sum of money and energy was wasted on this project when it could have been used for something productive. She had difficulty in finding the parts to replace some of the equipment. The Master answered that it was done for you to accept and believe in the reality of our existence in your lives. He said that the group present at her house was all new to this manner of teaching and the impact of the presence of the Masters. They all wanted proof. The event was given to bring proof that indeed the power of the Masters can influence your life and even your homes and electrical equipment. Those pieces of the equipment which had not been repaired were there to be a reminder of the event, and now that the belief had been established, they would be repaired and the monies would be brought back by the grace of the Masters. The Masters do have great compassion for us, but they will have no problems making a point where necessary. Remember, therefore, to say the invocation for the equipment!

In one of my early encounters with Thoth, I asked him to take his mask of the Ibis bird off. He told me that I wouldn't be able to bear his gaze. This made me more curious and more determined to continue to ask him. Finally, he did take it off, I looked into his eyes which looked like the clearest and the deepest of oceans. Looking through the window of his soul, he touched my heart, and I melted in the love I felt pouring out for all humankind. His love has no bounds and his power seems equally as great, at least from our human standpoint. Enjoy the light and the intensity of his energies through the following pages.

Connection to the Cosmic Sun

Commentary: This is a very important journey that Thoth is offering us. In this journey he first requests and receives the dispensation to create a rite of passage to visit the Palace of Shamballa. Then we go to the initiation chamber and receive the Pure White Light, the original blueprint of divine self and to commune with the male and female aspects of the Kumaras.

He then requests on our behalf and is granted the dispensation to offer everyone the purification and removal of pain and dross of eons of lifetimes through the transmutational power of Violet Flame. He asks that this be in effect for as long as is necessary in order to bring us to one hundred percent pure light capacity through the downloading of original pure white blueprint. This is a feat absolutely unheard of in the scheme of dispensations, because one hundred percent pure light can only be granted to the initiates at the fifth level, the level of resurrection. Please note that he is asking for the dispensation that such quotients of light be given. To be given it is one thing, to receive it, fully embody it and maintain it long enough to become one hundred percent pure white light is completely a different matter. We will have to work to maintain such levels of light. That work requires discipline to purify the body, mind and spirit and willingness to stay in the pure state. It also requires that we continuously exercise this meditation to maintain the level of light and purity and to release impurities with the help of the Masters. Nevertheless, he is setting the pace and paving the path for this to become a reality, which members of our generation of souls or those who come after us can attain.

He also requests on our behalf that the removal of past pains be done without going through the mental and emotional process of clearing and the subsequent pain of remembering the trauma, which is generally the norm. This meditational journey and the decrees of intention within it are extremely powerful, and they can completely change your life and accelerate your spiritual growth and the evolution of your soul.

MASTER THOTH, CHANNELED JULY 1, 2003

Adonai, Adonai, Adonai. I stand at your feet with great love. I am Thoth. Take a deep breath with me.

I offer to make a pathway directing you to the retreat in Venus, the abode of the Kumaras, in Shamballa. First I make a pathway around your body, mind, emotions, thoughtforms, etheric and auric energy fields. Feel your energy field extending and expanding. Feel a sphere of light 30 feet in diameter spinning pure white light from Shamballa in Venus to encompass you. To create the light fields, I will pull a cylinder of light from Shamballa on Venus down to the crust of the Earth and around each one of you.

I also pull this cylinder of light to the heartcore of Mother Earth. What you hear is the heartbeat of Mother Earth. In the ancient traditions of the old people of Earth — those from the five corners that you call the Native or the Aboriginal people of Earth — permission is always requested before, during and after every ceremony from Mother Earth by entering into the heartcore of Mother Earth. The space of illumined light which is known as the heartcore of Mother Earth is connected directly to the heartcore of the God Flame — to the heartcore of the Undifferentiated Source — that part of Mother/Father God who has never taken form, never manifested itself physically and is above and beyond physical matter. The heartcore of Mother Earth maintains that connection to the heartcore of the Undifferentiated Source.

As you are extending and expanding your energy field outward, be sure to connect your own heartcore to the heartcore of Mother Earth. She, in turn, will take your offering (the heart connection) directly to the heart-flame that burns within the heartcore of the Undifferentiated Source, All That Is. See the cylinder of light become more illumined in light. Visualize the vibration of 100 percent pure white light become more intense within and around you, spinning and spiraling, into your heartcore, pulsing from your heart outward, connecting to the heartcore of Mother Earth, from the heartcore of Mother Earth to the heartcore of Shamballa on Venus, to the seven male and female Beings of Light, the Kumaras. Visualize the pure white light spinning and spiraling, expanding wider and brighter, from Venus through the Sun of the solar system, through the heartcore of the central Sun of the galaxy, through the heartcore of the Cosmic Sun, to the heartcore of Alpha and Omega, the great deities of the Sun of your Cosmos.

Pause, take a deep breath and feel the energies at the final destination in the center of the cosmic sun. Meditate on these energies for a moment.

Now we begin the return journey. Bring that vibration of light back through the same channels, through the same cylinder, spiraling from the heartcore of the Alpha Omega in the great Cosmic Central Sun, through the levels and layers of the Cosmos into your own Solar Sun, to the presence of Lord Helios and Lady Vesta, the deities of the Sun. It is fully intensified, as it returns to the light on Venus, magnifying the light on Venus, returning to the heartcore of the Kumaras. From the heartcore of the Kumaras and the flame of Venus to the heartcore of Mother Earth. From the heartcore of Mother Earth, with great blessing and love, it brings healing and wholeness to your own heartcore.

You do for yourself and the entire planetary grid. The joy is magnified to that intensity. If you feel pain, it is because you become the catalyst to remove the pain from the planet and the masses in order to unburden Earth and humankind. The pain at times may feel like more than one person could bear, and yet together we make an agreement: joy, peace and harmony will abound on the new Earth. It is only a matter of time.

For your own peace of mind, ask for a specific sign to be given to you. You can be as specific as you like or you can just say, *"Give me a sign that would remove my doubt and would give me the courage to walk this path, a sign that would give me even greater determination to walk this path. Give me hope. Give me joy that in a tangible world of dualities, I truly am making a difference."* And then see for yourself.

Sometimes it is beneficial to ask for something tangible to guide you upon your path, to give you hope, to help you focus your intention and your attention on the brighter horizons that are within reach and yet may seem far away. Ask for a personal sign if you wish it. Ask for the sign when you reach the heartcore of Mother Earth and unite your heart with her. Ask for a sign again when you reach the presence of the great central sun of the cosmos, Alpha and Omega. Ask yet again on your return journey when you arrive at the sun of your own solar system in the presence of Lord Helios and Lady Vesta. Ask for encouragement, hope, peace and harmony to walk on this path of straight and narrow. Take a deep breath.

The Kumara Twin Flames

Come with me now. Allow yourself to spin in the cylindrical white light tunnel (previous exercise), by first moving outwards through your crown chakra, follow your golden silver cord of light at the top of your head, the antahkarana, to the Presence of The I AM. (There is a cord of light that connects us from the top of our head, which is our seventh chakra, to our twelfth chakra where our presence of the I AM THAT I AM — God in form — resides.)

Let us call upon the I AM THAT I AM, to protect you and assist you to attain the highest and brightest essence of pure white light on this journey. Let us call upon the legions and hosts of angelic forces of light to protect your physical body while your spirit is on this journey. Through the golden silver cord of light, together we join the golden gate of the synchronic lines that bring us to the sacred Temple of Shamballa on Venus (synchronic lines are like highways of light in the etheric realms).

177

Upon entry through the golden gateway you are in the Great Hall meeting with the seven female and male Light Beings (the cosmic female and male aspects). These are the seven pairs of the Kumaras which form the male and female counterpart. Each one of you has a connection with one of the seven pairs. You will walk in a procession through an archway of light with the male Kumara to your left and the female Kumara to your right. The pair of Kumaras holds your hands and walks you through the illumined archway to a golden doorway into an initiation chamber of light. Inside that chamber you may communicate, request or offer whatever your heart desires. Ask for a boon from the male/female pair. Offer a prayer, personal or global. Say what you wish and pause to receive. Take a deep breath.

An initiation of light is now performed to your essence, giving you a rite of passage to visit this abode of light whenever you choose to request it. This is performed by the pair of Kumaras, male and female. You may request this encounter again and again during dreamtime, in meditation or in your fully awakened state while performing daily activities. It will not interfere with your daily life. You do not have to be in mediation to receive the illumined light from Shamballa through the presence of the male and female essence of the Kumaras who have established an illumined light connection with you. However, consciously you can attain more when you allow yourself to sit in meditation or before retiring and falling asleep.

The benefits will be awarded to you merely for the asking. It is the same when you call upon the Consuming Violet Flame. By divine right, when you ask, you do receive. Whether you consciously become aware of its impact, or physically feel the energetic encounter does not matter. When the cause is transmuted it will remove all effect and return you to your original blueprint as light. When you call upon The Consuming Violet Flame, the Violet Flame of Transmutation or the Purple Ray, because you have asked it is decreed to you. It is given whether you fully and tangibly or energetically feel it or not.

You are now given the rite of passage to enter into the initiation chamber in Shamballa and to request the initiation blaze of white light and a communion with the male and female pair of the Kumaras who have established a light connection with you. You can set up a decree that a transmission of this light be given to you at a certain time, in a certain manner. You can make a general intention to receive every hour on the hour. You can even make that intention to be with every breath, the blazing white fire of initiation to be administered to you until you become a hundred percent pure white light. Pause for a moment and state your intention. Call upon the Consuming Violet Flame to remove the pain and dross that your spirit and your soul have encountered in many lifetimes in the physical body of matter, enabling the return to the original blueprint of pure white light.

The advantage of removing the dross and the pain with the Violet Flame is that you do not have to bring to the surface of your consciousness every event to be transmuted and the scars to be released. You can relieve yourself from the pain and dross through the transmutational potencies of the Consuming Violet Flame merely by calling the Consuming Violet Flame. You can make a general intention for the release to happen with every breath. This dispensation is given to you who are the pioneers, spearheads, torchbearers and way-showers.

The original blueprint of a hundred percent pure white light can be established through your bodies, upon this globe, illuminating the grid of the 100 percent pure white light original blueprint on Earth for the benefit of all humankind. The more you focus your intention on the illumination of this global grid, the faster the process can be established.

As for yourselves, you have been given the rite of passage, you have been offered by your request that with every breath in and every breath out you will receive the higher light. And that you will transmute through the Consuming Violet Flame the pain and the dross and the scars of the eons of time. The more intently and intensely that you focus upon the same for yourself and for the globe, the faster the process can be accelerated. One voice can go so far. Ten voices together can go further. A hundred can take it even further. A few million would reach critical mass. We can begin with one voice. We can begin with one individual voice, and together we begin with one group voice.

The rite of passage has been established. If you so choose, you can specifically ask this male and female being to give to you a name by which you can call upon them. Take a deep breath. Move to their energies and ask for a name, a symbol, a signal to communicate with this cosmic pair and to feel their presence with you. Meditate. If you have not received a name, patiently ask again in your future encounters. It will be given to you. Once you have it, use it wisely, for the benefit of light, in service to light, in advancement of light. For you are 100 percent pure white light, and it is your divine right to demand it, to command it, to decree it and to become it.

Let us offer a prayer of thanksgiving and blessing to the Kumaras who have received you. As we part company, moving back to the Great Hall, reentering through the archway this time, the male being is on your right and the female being is on your left. You move under the same archway greeting each individual pair, returning to the golden gate on our journey homebound, through the golden silver cord of light to the crown chakra. If you are experiencing pressure headaches or neck pains, stomach upset or nausea now, request that these pains be removed by the Masters. Let your spirit essence which has been purified, cleansed and infused with pure white light return to your physical body. And sit in peace for a moment as your body and all aspects of your personality receive the illumined light.

I stand with great joy in your love and in your presence as your friend, your guide, your teacher and your companion on the pathway of light. I am Tahuti. Adonai.

Viewing the Solar System From Space

Commentary: In this exercise, Thoth holds us suspended in space to show us the view of Earth, Mercury, Neptune, Saturn and Jupiter as well as Venus. As I have explained in the introduction to Thoth, in his incarnation as the god Mercury, he was the deity of the planet Mercury and was involved in the evolution of all the planets and laws governing the planets and all souls. The Greeks called him Hermes. He brought the knowledge of Hermetica to Earth from that level. Hermetica is the wisdom of the gods and the mysteries of magical knowledge such as alchemy and eternal life. In this meditation Thoth brings us to the presence of Goddess Venus, the guardian of the planet Venus.

Known by the Greeks as Aphrodite, she is the Goddess of love and beauty. Worshipped in Rome as Venus, she is the Goddess of Love and Fertility as the ancestor to the Romans. As Venus Felix she is bringer of good fortune, as Venus Victrix, the bringer of victory and as Venus Verticordia, the protector of feminine chastity. Venus is also a nature goddess in charge of the spring season and the bringer of joy to humankind. Many nude statues of Venus have been sculpted by artists, yet as Venus Pompeiana, the patron deity of Pompeii, she wears a crown and is fully clothed. Sanat Kumara's encounter with Venus in Janet McClure's book gives an account of a great cosmic being filled with love of the highest caliber. Her essence permeates everywhere on Venus. All initiates of the twelve Temples of Wisdom, where training for planetary and galactic service is given, receive her love and are nurtured by it. Thoth brings us back to Atlantis to retrieve the secret mysteries from that era before he brings us back to full consciousness of our bodies on Earth.

MASTER THOTH, CHANNELED OCTOBER 12, 2003

Beloveds, Adonai, Adonai. I am Thoth. Take a deep breath.

Prepare your bodies by envisioning one pillar of light extending from the bottom of each of your feet into the crust of the Earth, into the body of Mother Earth, to the core crystalline structure in the heart of Mother Earth. The Sun that shines in that heartcore welcomes you and holds you grounded.

Envision from the top of your head your cord of antahkarana extending your life force to your soul. Moving through your entire soul lineage, you become aware of the hierarchies of the self, the Higher Self, the presence of your own I AM. From there you move to the presence of the Elohim, the energy field of the Throne of Grace, and finally to the presence of the Undifferentiated Source, All That Is within the void. Envision the Great Central Sun of this entire Cosmic Constellation at the heart of the Void. Envision wrapping the antahkarana around a crystalline structure like the disk of a sun, and wrap the antahkarana around this disk inside the heart of the central sun. Now you are connected through your lineages of light and your own soul structure to the spirit of oneness. From this viewpoint, look at the planet Earth within the solar system. Now look at the Sun. Feel the love and the warmth that comes to you from the Sun.

Now become aware of the planet Mercury, where many of the high level initiates are gathered. Hierarchies of the Ascended Beings of Light and even the cosmic beings of light have made Mercury their homes. Become aware of planet Neptune, very far away from your own planet. Feel the energy vibration of this planet. Bless it and love it and feel the love returned to you. Become aware of planet Saturn, a very large planet with many levels and layers of rings around it. Feel the energy vibration from this planet. Become aware of planet Jupiter. This is a very highly evolved planet in your own star system. Its energy is very similar to the energy of the Sun, only gentler and not quite as bright. But nevertheless, it is far, far advanced in the levels of planetary mastery. Now become aware of Venus. Venus has a purple light structure around it, a mixture of emerald green and purple. This energy field around Venus is somewhat similar to the energy field that the Children of the New Age bring forth to Earth. It brings healing and order to life.

Many children, especially those born since August of 2002, have auric fields of exactly these colors, and many are destined to become healers. The green relates to the Fifth Ray, the Ray of Truth, and the purple relates to the Seventh Ray, the Ray of Transmutation of Dross and Return to Purity, also the Ray representing Ceremonial Order. These children come to Earth on this specific Ray to bring order to the Aquarian Age. They come to heal the planet and the multitudes and masses of souls.

Goddess Venus, The Cosmic Guardian

I would now like to present to you the presence of the Cosmic Being Venus. See this wondrous Cosmic Being of Light standing in the center of a circle. She is very tall, somewhat slender, although very feminine. Look into her eyes. It is as though you are looking into the depths of the ocean. She has very big almond-shaped eyes. As strong as these eyes are, they are innocent, as innocent as looking into the eyes of a newborn baby.

Look at her attire. These gossamer garments of light are normal attire in the retreat of Shamballa on Venus. These garments of light protect the wearer from lower forces and transmit the higher vibration of light to the environment around them. It is as though she is illuminating the room, and her garments are lit. Yet the garment itself is transparent.

Become aware of her hands. She is holding her hand in a certain position. Her right hand, palm up, is facing your heart. Her left hand, palm down with the back of the hand showing, is pointing to your solar plexus and sacral plexus area. A beam of light is emanating from her right hand. The color is a bluish-white. The beam of light emanating from the left hand is a golden-yellow-orange color. Absorb and receive these energies. Take a deep breath.

As the beams of light reach within your body, they expand; the beam of golden-yellow and orange spreads in the area of the hip and the stomach, and the beam of bluish-white spreads in the entire chest area. The beams reach toward each other mixing and merging, and they unite in a pure white light in the area above the solar plexus, close to the bottom rib. A vortex of light is created in that area. This is where the Soul is in residence. This is the Seat of the Soul.

When complete awareness of divinity exists, this light resides on the right side of your chest. When complete awareness is yet missing this vibration falls down below the cosmic heart and even below the human heart, hiding itself under the ribcage, sitting on top of your diaphragm. When facing trauma or in an anxiety attack, the breath is imprisoned, not reaching the core of the body, and you may begin to hyperventilate. In those circumstances, the pain and suffering affects the Seat of the Soul and causes the contraction of the diaphragm, which interferes with your normal breathing process leading to hyperventilation or shallow breathing. Over many instances of trauma you become numb to this abnormality. With these beams of light permeating the area, healing will ensue.

Feel the warmth of the two rays in your body as beloved Venus continues to send healing. Allow your being to absorb these energies. Ask the Goddess to heal all trauma and to release all pain so you can begin to breathe deeply again. From now on, in anxious moments remember to call upon Cosmic Being Venus. After any anxious or traumatic moment, request the restoration of your breathing through the emanation of the light from her hands. Pause and take a deep breath.

Now become aware that a beam of pink light is emanating from her heart, shooting out directly to your own cosmic heart chakra in the area of your thymus gland, spreading in your chest, throat, neck, and shoulders. Take a deep breath and absorb the pink light of divine love emanating from the heart of Venus to your own heart, and make the intention to release all pain, depression, hopelessness and fear. Ask for the restoration — to perfection — of the plan in your own heart. Ask for the perfected divine plan and the original blueprint to imprint at cellular level in the cosmic heart. Ask for the connection from your own heart to the cosmic heart of the Central Sun of this Cosmos. If you wish, using your own free will request that this connection never be severed ever again. Pause and take a deep breath.

From this moment on, you are connected to the cosmic heart of the great central Sun. This is the highest source of your own beingness. It will guide you through Mastery and beyond — prepare you for communion with your own Lineage of Light, Soul group, sisters and brothers of light, teachers, guides and guardians. Connecting with the soul group members will bring you wholeness, a feeling you may have lacked for awhile. There is no one closer to you than members of your own soul group because your soul group has been with you through many lifetimes. It is highly probable that some are not in physical embodiments at this present moment. And those who are in body may not necessarily be in your life. In fact, the idea is that members of the soul group scatter in different parts of the world or the universe in order to learn from different experiences, in different circumstances, on different planets or star systems. However, there is nothing stopping you from joining and merging telepathically with members of your own soul group. Therefore if you wish it, put in the intention that at nighttime or at any other time where you are in a relaxed, meditative mode a reconnection with your own soul group members would take place.

It is now time to have one final experience with the Cosmic Being Goddess Venus. She offers you to step into her body, stand inside of her and merge and join into her beingness, allowing your own beingness to be imbued by her cosmic vibration of light. Do this with your own free will and with great love and sincerity. As you join and merge and expand inside her cosmic being, your own cell struc-ture become lighter, the atoms in your body vibrate faster, your electronic structure become recalibrated and your body and being fill up with Pure White Light, the bluish-white light which is her signature light. Take a deep breath and visualize yourself fully and completely merged into the pres-ence of the Goddess Venus. Expand into her beingness and receive from the pure essence of this cosmic being of light. Meditate for a while and return to your normal con-sciousness when you are ready.

Return To Atlantis — Union With Twin Flame

From here I take you back to Atlantis. Along the way I bring you to the cave of the mysteries. In this embodiment you will be in a better position to absorb those mysteries. As we enter into the cave, the writing on the walls of the cave come to life and begin emanating different colored light. And as you look down at your own body, you will see that the corresponding point of light in your own body is illuminated. This exercise will help to activate the memories of the great knowledge and wisdom which existed in those times. Your own being is reactivated to absorb those mysteries and recall the knowledge and wisdom once again. The awakening of the memories of the mysteries in your own body will assist in transmission of these energies back to Earth at the present time. This is why I bring you here. You are drawn to the different parts of the cave. There are many walls, many labyrinths. You are called to places where specific knowledge and wisdom is transmitted through the illumination of lights into your bodies. Pause and take a deep breath.

We will exit from a different point than the one we entered. This exit point is a crack in the time-space continuum and will directly guide us to the Temple of Atlantis. You will find yourself standing in the center of the Golden Temple around a pyramid-shaped structure. You begin to emanate from your third eye and the palms of your hands, and the pyramid disappears. You then enter and move to an inner chamber of light to receive your own guidance and revelations. A being who is your counterpart — or your Twin Flame — from that time is awaiting you. In the presence of this being we will continue this journey in silence. You will receive your initiation, and you will return to me for our journey back to Earth. Pause and take a deep breath.

Let us bless the presence of all these beings of light. Let us be thankful for all the merits that we have earned on this auspicious day. You are now beacons of light transmitting this light. You have the choice to anchor these energies consciously, vibrate them to others, decree and command these lights to reign on Earth. You have the divine right to choose this with your own free will. Pause and make your intention.

Now, I take you back. Together we bring the energies of the Mayan, the Egyptian and the Atlantean civilizations. Together we pave the path of light that will remain open to all those who wish to benefit from these energies, provided their intention is pure light and service of light. Together we have become the bridge. Together we have become the pillars of light that hold this bridge together. This bridge extends from this present moment in Earth's history to the Atlantean era with a stop to create a double arch to form the coming together of the Mayan, Aztec, Egyptian and Aboriginal energies of Australia and New Zealand. We will replenish these energies with the Lemurian light of wisdom. A vortex of light will open up to bring energies from that civilization. You can invoke and awaken this moment in time and space by practicing to reconnect with the high point of the Lemurian civilization.

With great love and in thanksgiving, I call the completion and culmination of this session of communion. I bless you; I stay with you for as long as necessary until we have completed the last phase of the last job at hand or in the future. I am Thoth. Adonai. Adonai. Adonai. So it is.

Soul Lineage of Light

Synopsis

1. Every human being on Earth has a Soul Lineage of Light. This is the soul's family tree or history. It is a family roster which Metatron calls the soul lineage of Light. That family stays the same from one incarnation to the next. (This only discusses the soul's lineage. The personality aspect and the land in which a human incarnates have their own family history.)

2. The Soul Lineage was formed when the Pure White Light descended from the heart of God, The Undifferentiated Source, and entered into the realm of matter. In its descent to matter, it slowed down. As matter became solidified, it offered greater resistance to the Pure White Light, causing it to fracture as though going through a prism.

3. From the fracture came the Seven Rays similar to but not exactly the same as the seven colors of the rainbow.

4. Each Ray carries a quality. These qualities were given to the Rays by the Seven Mighty Elohim, who are the architects and builders of our universe.

5. When souls began to take bodies of matter, they chose one of these Seven Rays and its quality to represent them (somewhat like being born into the Smith family in England or the Zulu tribe in Africa). A soul adopts the quality attributed to their chosen Ray.

6. In each incarnation we choose a different personality who is ruling over the body. That personality also comes to Earth on a Ray called the Personality Ray. The Personality Ray and the Soul Ray are not the same. Although beyond the scope of this book, Alice Bailey

and Benjamin Crème discuss these in great detail (see Cited Works).

7. On Earth, each Ray has an Ascended Master called a Chohan supervising it and an Archangelic force with its legions guarding and protecting the souls on that Ray. When you consciously connect with your Ray of Light, you work with the Master directly and know the Angelic Forces who guard you. It is important for every human being on the spiritual path to come into contact with their soul lineage, their guides, their Angelic Forces and the Ascended Master Chohan for their Ray. Finding the Soul Ray, understanding the qualities of the Ray and using the colors of the Ray for healing and protection are of great importance for raising the Soul consciousness. The nature of the Soul is hidden from the consciousness and personality until you discover your Soul Lineage and Ray. Like an orphaned child who suddenly finds a loving family, finding our soul lineage of Light is like reuniting with loving family members we had not known before or not seen in a very long time.

The following offers a more detailed explanation of each Ray and its qualities. It is also a map to introduce you to the Seven Mighty Elohim who brought the Rays and their qualities to manifest form. The Seven Chohan and the Seven Angelic Forces are great guides and friends that you have (knowingly or unknowingly) worked with for eons of time. Coming into conscious contact with these beings helps connect you with your own Higher Self.

Introduction and Invocation

BALDUINSTEIN GERMANY, FEBRUARY 2, 2005

In the name of the I AM THAT I AM, I call forth the pillar of Pure White Light and the Presence of the I AM THAT I AM, and I ask that the information given herein be brought from the highest truth and the Purest of White Light. I ask the Presence of THE I AM THAT I AM to be the witness to these truths. I call forth the presence of Christ Maitreya and Sanat Kumara to guide the transmission and reception of these materials.

The following material is a collection of teachings that I have researched and also received directly from the Masters over many years. For the most part, I receive the information in this way: one of the Masters of Wisdom or the Ascended Beings of Light comes forward explaining certain truths and mysteries. Shortly thereafter, I come to find other materials that correspond to the information that I have received directly. Over time, the information expands, and all the pieces of the puzzle come together.

Sometimes the Masters instruct me to write down the teachings. It is not easy to put the teachings into written form. When I am in those expanded states of consciousness, I find it much easier to absorb the teachings and understand their meaning. Putting that knowledge into words becomes very limiting and loses its expansive nature because we absorb words through the mind, and these teachings have to be absorbed and understood with the heart. Sometimes a concept needs to be explained to me in many different ways for the mind to fully absorb it before I can put it into words.

This is why some of the channeled information can be read more than once, and the reader gathers new information each time, receiving exactly what they need. As our spiritual wisdom and knowledge expands, the material can be absorbed and digested at a higher level. The information seems to have many layers of meaning. The same material takes on new meaning because we can absorb and understand it from a higher perspective.

There is another way that I receive information. Sometimes I begin to read relevant information and material in a book. While reading, I am taken on a journey to experience not only the information that is contained in the book but related material. In this way, the Masters explain the mysteries of the universe and what lies beyond the known territories. By allowing me to enter into the realms of the unknown, the Masters bring the knowledge and wisdom back to our realm of mundane reality. As Lord Metatron would put it, they map the unknown by bringing what is as yet invisible to the visible. When you reveal what is hidden in a dark corner, you can have a greater understanding of it. The Masters help me go into the invisible realms that lie behind the written words of a book and bring to focus and understanding the hidden meanings and the unknown truths. Then when I write about it, give a workshop or teach a class, along with everyone who has the experience, we map the unknown. I have presented the material on the soul lineage of Light because of the request from esoteric and metaphysical higher educational organizations who wish to include them as graduate and post-graduate college courses.

The material on the Soul Lineage of Light is somewhat complicated and requires great research and devotion to the subject. As you read through this material, please bear in mind that this is a very concentrated form of a large body of material. If you want to pursue this wisdom, please refer to Cited Works. Each paragraph of this portion is laden with the names, qualities and information relevant for an advanced student of metaphysics. Please do not be disheartened if you feel overwhelmed by it at first. The potency is there even when your consciousness cannot absorb all of it at once. Even though I have studied this material extensively and know these beings, I still need to refer to my notes when teaching a class on The Soul Lineage of Light. If this is your first intro-duction to much of this material, take heart and know that it is enough to simply read the name of a being. The energy will permeate into your own body and beingness. In time to come, you may begin to become conscious of working with one or many of these mighty beings and not even remember that your first introduction was through this book. My prayer and hope is that you will gain from it everything that the Masters and your guides deem necessary for you.

Allow yourself time to grow and process the teachings from the rest of this book and other materials. Great growth can occur in a short time. A friend who was given a copy of my first *Gifts* book called me seven months after her first reading of the book. She had taken it with her on a business trip and read the entire book cover to cover for the second time. She told me that she appreciated the material much more than the first time. When I asked her what had changed, she told me she had grown much during the course of the seven months. She was getting to know the beings energetically by invoking them and by reading other relevant materials. The first time reading the book whet her appetite; the second time she absorbed and digested it as though it were nectar. Each experience brings its own blessings.

I have worked with The Elohim, The Masters or Chohans of the Seven Rays and The Archangels extensively for years. At the turn of the century, Lord Metatron instructed me to give life readings to connect the recipients with their Main Primary Guides, The Masters of their Ray of Light, their Angelic Guardians and members of their own Soul Lineage. This helps people to discover their own origin, know their divine purpose and connect to the Ray of Light upon which they have come to Earth. (For details on life readings, go to www.nasrinsafai.com.)

In the course of the past two years, Christ Maitreya has instructed me to bring forth these teachings under the heading of "The Soul Lineage of Light." I now sit in Balduinstein, Germany, totally immersed in the Light of Mother Meera, a living avatar who is in residence in Schamburg. Mother Meera is here to invoke and bring down to Earth the energies of the Paramatman Light. Atman is the Pure Light of the Self — the Pure White Light of God-Self. Para means beyond. Paramatman is the Supreme Self or God Self. It is the Light of that high and bright nature that is beyond form and beyond individualization. It is beyond distinction and differentiation. To that Paramatman Light all shall return in purity and love.

The Creation of the Solar System

In the very beginning before even time existed, the Cosmic Consciousness we call God, The Undifferentiated Source, was sitting in total bliss of its beingness in the

195

silence of the Great Void. That Cosmic Consciousness chose of its own desire to experience beingness outside of the great silence. The command, or the Word, was sent out, "Let there be Light. Let me become many." From the heartcore of that great silence, the spark of Light was illuminated. Archangel Uriel received the spark of Light and became its keeper. That is known as the inner Light. Uriel brought the spark of Light from the heartcore of The Undifferentiated Source — God without form — to the surface of existence. Once at the surface, the spark became the outer Light. Through externalizing that Light, Archangel Metatron created all the manifest universes and beyond — everything in the worlds of form and matter, energy and existence, time and space.

Metatron first created the five sacred geometric shapes, better known as the plutonic solids. All lifeforms have their form and existence rooted in these sacred geometries. Even the length, width and measurements of our body parts (all body parts of all animals, birds, flowers, plants, etc.) are based on these sacred geometries. The journey of creation began when these sacred geometries entered into the time-space continuum.

The descent from the Light of the Cosmic Consciousness to the beingness that you and I are took many eons of time. From our point of view, it counts in billions of years. But then, from the point of Light where the Cosmic Consciousness Uriel and Metatron were sitting, time as we know it doesn't exist. The journey of descent starts at the Great Void and moves through 144 dimensions of reality to this third dimensional realm, where linear time and space create heavy densities of matter. As Light began to reach to the outer realms it slowed down and became heavy. Light became energy, energy condensed and became matter,

matter acquired mass, mass condensed and became heavy. (Through channelings, Metatron has given the above description of the 144 dimensions of reality. Some schools of metaphysics divide the levels or dimensions to 352 or 333 or other numbers. Please bear in mind that the vastness of these realms is beyond our imagination. Each of these systems are valid according to the division of the realms for each of those schools of thought and their teachings.)

Along the journey, Light moved from the heart of the great central sun of the cosmos where Alpha and Omega (the beginning and the ending) reside. Then it moved down to many omniverses, which are conglomerates of many universes. And further, down to our local universe where Lord Melchizedek and Lady Malak reside as our universal logos. Logos is a Greek word which means "The Word." The book of Genesis states, "In the beginning was the Word and the Word was with God. And the Word was God." The Word came descending from the heartcore of the cosmic source, gaining density during its descent. As the density thickened, Pure White Light began to go through the prism of differentiation. It fractured into the Seven Rays. These Seven Rays are the basis of the Soul Lineage of Light teachings. They become the source or the lineage for all souls in our universe.

These Seven Rays are active throughout our universe. We follow their path from our universe to our galaxy (Milky Way) down to our solar system and finally to Earth. Each of the Seven Rays would come into manifest form through the efforts of one set of Mighty Elohim. They are the architects who build and bring to manifestation the Rays and their qualities. Each of the Seven Rays (once condensed) became the main focus for great populations of souls who would come to bodies of matter carrying the qualities of the Ray. Souls would be protected by the Angelic Forces for that Ray and supervised by an Ascended Master or Chohan ("Master" or "wise being"). Chohan literally means "ancient" in Farsi. The Seven Chohans who together hold office over the Seven Rays are themselves under the supervision of one great Ascended Being called MahaChohan. Maha in Sanskrit means "highest." MahaChohan supervises The Seven Rays, Chohans, Angelic Forces and all the souls who come on each Ray. Metatron and Uriel hold either end of this spectrum: Outer and Inner LIGHT.

Metatron, as the holder of external Light, is the final force in a supervisory role over all of manifestation. Bear in mind that Metatron manifested this entire creation from the spark of Pure White Light which came from the heart of God, The Undifferentiated Source. When all the Seven Rays leave the duality and return to Pure White Light, Metatron will collect them and pull them back into Pure Light. The Pure White Light spark is then returned to its source by Archangel Uriel, the holder of inner Light or inner spark. Metatron is the being in charge of all the Rays, the Angelic Forces, the Chohans, MahaChohan and the Elohim.

Moving from the universal levels of Light, the Seven Rays descended through many galaxies to the heartcore of our own galaxy, the Milky Way. The guardians of this galaxy are Lord Melchior and Lady Melchai. The Light descended into the density from the galactic core to our own sun. At the level of our own sun, Lord Helios and Lady Vesta are the deities of our solar system. They held this Light in their own heart and dreamed the design of all the planets in the solar system. They mapped their design and presented it to the Councils of Light. (These councils are at solar, galactic and universal levels of decision making. All designs must be approved for manifestation by the relevant residing councils.) To help complete the project, The Great Cosmic Being known as The Silent Watcher was called forth. The Silent Watcher holds the design in her consciousness until the design can fully blossom and become physically manifest, which may take eons of time.

The Seven Mighty Elohim and the Seven Rays

I have used the names of the Mighty Elohim as given in the teachings of Geraldine Innocenti, compiled by Thomas Printz. Elizabeth and Mark Prophet of Summit Lighthouse Foundation use other names for some of the Mighty Elohim (see Cited Works).

For the design to come into full manifest form, the Seven Mighty pairs of Elohim, who are the architects of our universe, were called. Each of the seven pairs of Elohim then took it upon themselves to manifest one aspect or step of the creation of the solar system. The entire process is encapsulated in the seven properties that the Seven Mighty Elohim hold. The seven steps to bring forth this solar system into manifest form are:
1. The original idea and the design (quality of Original Intent or Will)
2. The illumination of the design (quality of Illumination or Wisdom)
3. The embodiment of the design in the Divine Love (quality of Divine Love)

4. The purity of intent and clarity of focus to manifest form (quality of Purity and Focus)
5. The concentration and consecration of manifested form (quality of Truth)
6. The peace and harmony to hold the form together (quality of Peace and Service)
7. The rhythm and pulse to maintain the manifest form in absolute order and organization (quality of order and organization as well as transmutation of negativity).

According to the *Book of Zohar*, the Elohim are the mighty forces of Light who can withstand the presence of God. Metatron says that the Elohim reside between the 52nd and the 144th dimension and can reach and withstand the highest intensity dimension, which is the Throne of God. God resides there as The Undifferentiated Source without need for form. The Elohim normally operate from that high intensity of Light all the way down to the 52nd dimension of reality, where non-form begins into move to semi-form. Below the 52nd, semi-form becomes even more dense. Between the 52nd and 13th are various levels of semi-form (ethereal form). At the 13th dimension, the I AM THAT I AM or God in Form resides. From here on down bodies of solid matter are formed. Ordinarily the Elohim would not descend lower than this level. Occasionally they make their presence felt to us and bring messages through channelings. In this book, you have experienced the energies of the Elohim of Peace and the Elohim of Illumination, Minerva. The Elohim have made a great sacrifice to enter into realms of solid form in order to help the creation of this solar system.

The word Elohim is the plural form for Eloha, which means "of El" or "of God." In this discourse, we will use the word Elohim even when we are speaking of a singular being. They are collective consciousnesses of extreme might and Light. Although they have taken male and female aspects to withstand the polarity of lower densities, they are whole in their entirety. Each set of the Mighty Elohim is in charge of one of the Seven Rays. The color of the Ray holds all the qualities of that Ray. Each Ray's qualities are held within a flame of that color.

The Seven-Fold Flame of the Seven Mighty Elohim

In *The Seven Mighty Elohim Speak* by Thomas Printz, the Lord MahaChohan states in regards to the Seven-Fold Flame, *" Upon the Forehead of every individualized God-intelligence there is a beautiful crown of Light, on the front of which are seven flames in the colors which represent the Seven Rays of the Elohim"* (p. xii) This crown is not visible to humankind but it may be clearly seen by those with true "inner sight" and by the cosmic beings, Ascended Masters and the Angelic host who minister to mankind. This crown is a natural God-gift of Light to every God-intelligence incarnated and is the anchorage of the Seven Rays of the Elohim in every brow.

We will now address the Seven Rays and their corresponding flames which constitute the Seven-Fold Flame discussed above. According to Metatron, a Ray represents the feminine aspect and the element of water. A flame represents the masculine aspect and carries the element of fire. An energy is the child aspect and represents the element of air, which is a Lighter element than the other two. There are

201

a total of five elements — Earth, Water, Fire, Air and Ether,- and with them all matter was made. Ether is the highest element and contains the other four.

The Seven Mighty Elohim Guarding the Seven Rays

RAY 1: Hercules and Amazon
The First Ray was given to Hercules and Amazon, the Elohim of the First Ray of the Divine Will of God. They are in charge of the ideal design for the manifestation of this solar system. The color is Aquamarine Blue. It is the first vibration of that Pure White Light after it moves through the prism of separation. The blue flame is the first plume of the Seven-Fold Flame of the Seven Mighty Elohim.

RAY 2: Cassiopia and Minerva
Cassiopia and Minerva are in charge of the Second Ray. They were to perceive the design and illuminate it for manifestation of the divine perspective. The color of the Second Ray is yellow, and the Yellow Flame is the second plume of the Seven-Fold Flame. The Second Ray-Flame quality is the Divine Wisdom.

RAY 3: Orion and Angelica
The Third Ray Elohim are Orion and Angelica. This Ray holds the Divine Love of God and is pink in color, making the third plume of the Seven-Fold Flame. The energies of these first three plumes represent the heavenly aspect of Light as it moves from non-manifest to manifest form.

RAY 4: Claire and Star Astrea
The Fourth Ray Elohim Claire and his female form Astrea, or Star Astrea, held the purity of the essence for creating the solar system. Their task was to maintain the purity of the original intention. The Fourth Ray is a crystalline white

Light, very close to the Pure White Light before separation. These Elohim are the bridge between the heavenly aspect — the manifestation of the first three Rays and the Earthly aspects — the manifestation of the last three Rays. The fourth plume of the Seven-Fold Flame is white.

RAY 5: Vista Cyclopea and Crystal

The Fifth Ray Elohim are Vista or Cyclopea, the male aspect, and Crystal. Their task was to concentrate and consecrate all manifest forms and to uphold Truth transferred from non-manifest to manifest form, and they materialized in bodies of matter. This they did through the living force of the Emerald Green Ray, the Ray of Truth and Healing. The fifth plume of the Seven-Fold Flame is emerald green.

RAY 6: Peace Tranquility and Pacifica

The male form of the Elohim of Peace is called Tranquility or Peace, and the female is Pacifica. Their task was to bring peace and devotional service; service to maintain all manifest form in creation. The Sixth Ray is Gold and Ruby-Red. Gold provides physical sustenance from the higher realms to the physical realm, and Ruby Red provides the life force from the Earthly realms to the heavenly realms. The sixth plume of the Seven-Fold Flame is golden ruby-red colored.

RAY 7: Arcturus and Diana

The last pair of Elohim are Arcturus and Diana. They bring Order into manifestation with the help of the Seventh Ray, the Ceremonial Order and The Violet Flame of Transmutation. This last Ray completes the journey from non-manifest to manifest and from spirit to matter. It is also the bridge from manifest to non-manifest and from matter to Pure White Light. For this reason, this last Ray is the Ray of Invocation for the Return to the Pure White Light. It is also the Ray of Transmutation of the dross and the pain of duality. It prepares the path for the return to God Unity and attainment of the Pure White Light. The seventh plume of the Seven-Fold Flame is purple.

Under the loving supervision of Lord Helios and Lady Vesta and the loving participation of the Great Silent Watcher and the Seven Mighty Elohim, the design came into manifest form. Each of the Seven Rays spread their Light under the supervision of a Chohan. Seven Great Beings were chosen from Ascended Masters to become the Chohans. At this point in the evolution of Earth, the seven Chohans are: Master El-Morya, Lord Lanto, Master Paul the Venetian, Serapis Bey, Master Hilarion, Master Lady Nada and Master St. Germain. For this evolutionary phase, each Ray was given a 14,000 year cycle of time to be anchored upon Earth. Once successfully anchored, those periods are considered as a Golden Age. The Grand Cycle for the Seven Golden Ages is 98,000 years.

CHOHAN 1: El-Morya
The first Golden Age brought the anchoring of the Blue Ray of the Divine Will of God. All the souls whose lineage of Light is the First Ray were called to Earth to assist in the anchoring of the first Golden Age. An archangel being of Light and its legions was then invited to be the angelic force guarding the first Golden Age. El-Morya is the Master Chohan of the First Ray, The Blue Ray of Divine Will of God, and this name he held in one of his incarnations on Earth in the Middle East. As Chohans are concerned, El-Morya is the longest-serving Master to this day. In another incarnation he was Shah Jahan, the great king who built the marble monument in Agra India known as the Taj Mahal. As the Great Persian King Akbar, he brought many of the religions of the world together and coined the phrase, "Alaho

Akbar" meaning "God is Great." The Archangelic force who is the guardian of the First Ray is Archangel Michael, which literally means, "In the likeness of God or the glory of God." He stands with his sword of mercy drawn out of its sheath, emanating blue Light, protecting and guarding all the souls of the First Ray.

CHOHAN 2: Master Lanto

The Chohan for the Second Ray is Lord Lanto. In a string of lifetimes in Lemuria, Lanto achieved great wisdom and evolved to great spiritual heights. As Lanto he was born in China and experienced its Golden Age. He holds the vibration of the Second Ray, the Wisdom to share with Earth. Lord Lanto achieved his Mastery while he was studying under Lord Himalaya, a great cosmic being residing over the Himalayan Mountain ranges. The Angelic Forces of Jophiel and its legions are here to protect the Second Ray souls.

CHOHAN 3: Master Paul the Venetian

The Chohan of the Third Ray is Master Paul the Venetian (Paolo Veronese), a master painter famous for his paintings of Christian saints. He expressed the energies of The Divine Love of God through his art and his open heart. According to the teachings of Mark and Elizabeth Clair Prophet in *Lords of the Seven Rays*, Master Paul served in the building of the civilization of Atlantis. He transferred the culture and established the Third Ray flame in Peru in anticipation of the sinking of the continent of Atlantis. The Archangelic force of the Third Ray is Archangel Chamuel. Archangel Chamuel and its legions guard the souls of the Pink Ray of Divine Love.

CHOHAN 4: Master Serapis Bey

The Chohan for the Fourth Ray, the Crystalline White Light of Purity, is Master Serapis Bey. He was a high priest in the Ascension Temple in Atlantis. He is very devoted to the Divine Mother, and he chose the White Ray in honor of

The Divine Mother. The angelic force that is guarding the Fourth Ray is Archangel Gabriel. Gabriel and its legions of Light are here as the messengers of God, holding the essence of Purity and Clarity for all the souls on the Fourth Ray.

CHOHAN 5: Master Hilarion

The Chohan of the Emerald Green Ray is Master Hilarion. In a previous lifetime he was Saint Paul, the apostle to Master Jesus. As an abbot monk called Hilarion, he became sainted by the church. The Archangelic force that holds the guardianship over the Fifth Ray is Archangel Raphael, the angel of healing, ministration, and music.

CHOHAN 6: Master Lady Nada

The Chohan for the Ray of Service is Master Lady Nada. She served in Atlantis as a priestess in the Temple of Love. She helps guide the children of the New Age (the Indigo children) and their parents. She also offers her assistance to the twin flames. Lady Nada ascended over 3,000 years ago. The angelic force of the Sixth Ray is Archangel Uriel, who is also the original keeper of the inner Light. From the union of the inner Light and the outer Light through the gold and ruby Rays, Archangel Uriel and the legions of Uriel are here to protect and guide the Sixth Ray souls.

CHOHAN 7: Master St. Germain

Ascended Master St. Germain is the Chohan of the Seventh Ray. In previous lifetimes, he was St. Joseph, the father of Jesus and Compt Du St. Germain, a French nobleman. He has been deeply involved in the Constitution of the United States of America and the anchoring of the I AM energies on the American continent. He has channeled important materials called the *I Am Discourses of St. Germain* to Godfre and Lotus Ray King. Archangel Zadkiel with its legions, serve the Indigo souls to bring the dawning of the Seventh Golden Age.

Golden Ages and the Divine Plan

The divine intent and the perfect design for the anchoring of The Seven Cycles would be a 98,000-year Grand Cycle. What follows is the story of this Grand Cycle.

The first three Golden Ages progressed as planned. The First Golden Age anchored the Ray of the Divine Will of God. The Chohan, Angelic forces and souls of the First Ray completed their mission on Earth and ascended. The Second Golden Age anchored the Ray of Divine Wisdom of God, and those working on the second Ray ascended. The Third Golden Age anchored the Divine Love of God and completing their mission, those working on the Third Ray ascended. Each of these were anchored in their appointed 14,000-year cycles.

However, mid-cycle in the Fourth Ray of Purity, there was a development in the solar system. Our neighbor planet Mars had a catastrophic event. The occupant souls of the third dimensional reality of Mars caused the destruction and demise of that realm. Disembodied souls, without a third-dimensional planet to incarnate upon, began crowding our solar system and polluting the environment of the neighboring planets. Since the evolution of Earth was moving perfectly according to the divine plan, it was decided by the Karmic Board and the Councils of Light that Earth could be the recipient of these disembodied souls. From the mixing of these impure souls with the souls of the Fourth Ray, the evolution and the anchoring of the Fourth Ray — the crystalline white Ray of Purity —was delayed. When its 14,000 year cycle ended, few Fourth Ray souls managed to ascend, and the fourth Golden Age remained incomplete. With no mass ascension, the Fourth Ray souls remained on Earth to continue to evolve.

However, as the divine plan had to proceed, the Fifth Ray souls arrived at their appointed time. What was to be the full domain of the Fifth Ray souls had to be shared with the remaining population of the Fourth Ray. The Earth began to experience itself expanding to host more souls than originally intended. The Fifth Ray souls, whose task it was to bring the Ray of Truth and Hope and the emerald green Ray of Healing and Instant Manifestation, arrived on Earth unable to complete their task. The responsibility of concentration and consecration to the truth of God began from an unclean slate in a polluted environment. When the 14,000 years for the completion of the Fifth cycle came, the souls were unable to fully accomplish their task. A small number of highly-evolved souls were able to make their ascension individually. These souls were able to maintain the truth by concentrating and consecrating themselves to the Fifth Ray. The Fifth Ray souls, the Chohan, and the Archangelic Forces remained on Earth.

The time for the entry of the Sixth Ray souls approached. The energies of peace, harmony and divine service to the Light were brought to Earth amidst great pollution and overpopulation. The Fourth and Fifth Ray souls were still awaiting their Ascension. The problems intensified with the entry of the Sixth Ray souls. Their purpose shifted from Divine Service to serving the souls of previous Rays. Too many cycles of incarnation beyond allotted time caused greater karmic entanglements for the Fourth, the Fifth, and now the Sixth Ray souls. Unable to accomplish their task of Divine Service, the Chohan, the Angelic Forces, and almost all the Sixth Ray souls remained on Earth. Archangel Michael, along with the Chohans of all the previous Rays and other Angelic Forces, came back to the rescue of Earth.

At this present moment in the evolution of the souls and planet Earth, we are entering into the seventh and final phase of this Grand Cycle, which would have ordinarily borne seven Golden Ages. The Earth is greatly overpopulated and immensely polluted. The Age of Pisces (6th cycle) has closed its doors, and the Age of Aquarius (7th cycle) has opened its gateways. The dawning of the seventh Golden Age is upon us. The Seventh Ray souls, which are of the highest sensitivity and require the greatest purity for their descent to Earth, are here. These are the souls known in New Age circles as the Indigo children, Crystal children, and Star children.

Over the scope of each Grand Cycle (98,000 years), the last 14,000-year cycle is the most important one. It is not only the ending of one Grand Cycle, but it also sets the pace for the beginning of the next Grand Cycle. The most highly evolved souls arrive from the four corners of the universe, because it is up to these souls to pioneer the return to the Pure White Light. The First Ray souls holding the Divine Will of God are the most determined, the most grounded and the most ancient of souls. The Seventh Ray Souls are the most other-worldly, the most sensitive, the most pure and hold the highest and brightest of Light. They require an environment that has been purified and elevated through the completion of all the six cycles before it.

In a perfect Grand Cycle, life would move according to the Original Intent and the Divine Plan. Therefore the First, Second and Third Rays would already be anchored and established. The Heavens would have already been brought to Earth. The bridge between Heaven and Earth, hosted by the Fourth Ray, would have been built. The Fifth Ray and the Sixth Ray would have been anchored. Upon such a solid foundation, the Seventh Ray souls would then enter the arena to bring order and organization. Through the Transmutation of All Dross and Invocation of the Pure White Light, the inner spark of God would be ignited with the help of Archangel Uriel, the Angelic Force of the Seventh Ray and Archangel Metatron to guide the reentry of souls to God Unity. The energies of the external Light return to the inner Light, and that Light returns to the beingness of the Cosmic Consciousness in the great void or great silence.

The pure Seventh Ray souls arrive and are faced with a polluted atmosphere. Breathing the air for them is like breathing poisonous gases. Living in the environment of untruth is like living in contaminated waste filled with contagious germs. Eating the polluted food is poisoning their bodies. Living in the mental chaos — rampant deception and greed, selfishness and forgetfulness — is poison to their minds. Imagine the plight of these souls — the highly evolved souls of the Seventh Ray — as they have started coming onto the Earth in preparation for the dawning of the Seventh Golden Age. Metatron and Quan Yin, in various channelings through me, have said that the first Indigo children arrived around 1972, with more coming in the 1980's and '90's. Almost all the children born since 2002 are Seventh Ray souls. Some of the early arrivals are now young adults.

Mass Ascension has not happened since the Third Ray souls completed their course 42,000 years ago. Attaining Mastery, which is the level before Ascension, is only happening on an individual basis. There are no schools where levels of Mastery, methodology, techniques or the science of Ascension and evolution of souls is taught anywhere openly on Earth. Mystery Schools and Mystic Philosophy Teachings, known to be the ultimate higher education in the course of the first three cycles and part of the fourth, are virtually nonexistent. The Masters who are in service to Light and the Ascended Masters of Light have devised programs and measures in order to change the course of events and bring forth remedial action. Ascension, the ultimate objective, can only be achieved when individual souls realize it as such. They must choose of their own accord to walk that path and find means to attain Mastery. When enough human beings in physical embodiment walk the path of Light and master their bodies, emotions, minds and souls we can complete this cycle. In order to overcome human needs, move beyond desires and release the struggles, humankind must find ways to live life in service to the Light. Then the Ascended Beings of Light can intercede on behalf of humanity, using the pioneer souls who choose Mastery to anchor the Light and change the course of events.

Some of the Masters of the Seven Rays who have been in service for a long time have moved from their position in service of the Rays to higher levels, creating stairways and hierarchies to make evolution to the higher realms of Ascension possible for individuals. Master Kut-humi moved from the Second Ray together with Master Jesus, previously Chohan of the Sixth Ray, to hold the office of the Christ. The office of the Christ is a stage in the levels of evolution where Light and teachings of Mastery are brought to every soul wishing to attain. Through attaining the Christed Self, and thereby initiation into the first and second levels, every human being will attain the consciousness of the true Self. Self-realization happens, and Mastery is attained as a result.

Above the office of the Christ is the office of the World Teacher. Christ Maitreya is that teacher. Maitreya means "the Buddha yet to come." The office of the Christ Maitreya is held by the one Supreme Being whose presence denotes the second coming of the Christ by the Christians, the return of Maitreya or Buddha by the Buddhists, the coming of the Savior by the Jews, the return of Krishna by the Hindus, the return of Imam Mahdi by Muslims and all other faiths who believe in the return of the Chosen One. Christ Maitreya has chosen to return to Earth to bring forth the coming of the 1000 Years of Peace. Metatron set the entry point for the 1000 Years of Peace as Spring Equinox, March 20-21, 2005. He also has informed us that the Masters of Light and Wisdom, under the leadership of Christ Maitreya, are preparing the multitudes of souls to receive mass initiation to the first level of spiritual awakening by August 12, 2005.

Christ Maitreya is here on Earth to assist in the mass opening of the heart chakra (the center for emotions) of the multitudes and masses. With his Light, Christ Maitreya will ignite the spark of the pure Self, infuse our bodies, our minds, our emotions, our souls and our spirits with the Divine Spark. Ignition of the Divine Spark will create the momentum to achieve critical mass, leading the entire population of Earth to awaken to their spirituality. From that awakening the Masters will guide us to infuse all the Seven Rays back with Pure White Light of the I AM.

Our soul lineage of Light can then fully accomplish and conclude its journey, returning from the Seven Rays to the Pure White Light. And from the Pure White Light to Oneness at the heartcore of the Undifferentiated Source, quiet and still.

In the stillness of total being, where all is ONE and ONE is All. So it is.

Acknowledgements

Many thanks to Susan Batchelder for her undivided attention, her undying Love and reverence for The Masters and this work, and for all the joy we shared through the process. And for compilation, editing, draft reviews, and great support in meeting deadlines and putting out all fires with great finess. To Ben Yates for his constructive editorial comments and contribution to transcriptions and diagrams. To Kathy Zaltash and Shara Shirvani for reviews and critiques. To Ronna Herman and Karen Bosch of Star Quest Publishing for cover design, book layout, printshop interface and distribution support, providing a publishing service dedicated to the evolution of consciousness and the production of Spirit, To Toni Maria Pinhiero for review and formatting; and to Michael Kopel for technical support, software, hardware, storing computer files and creating archives that will be kept for posterity. Because of his diligent work in archiving all tapes into sound files, we are now able to turn the transcripts of readings into book form. Thank you Michael! To Jim Foster for his support and witty remarks in the Foreword. To Victoria Kahari for all that she has taught me about writing and publishing books, and to her editorial and design team for the first *Gifts* book, Denise Khan and Kathleen Speers. To Denise for her support and love over many years and many lifetimes of performing austerities on the path of service.

Thanks to all the loved ones who have assisted in transcribing the readings and discourses, and those who participated in receiving the information which appears in this book. These wonderful souls attended classes, workshops, group channelings, held the energy for ceremonies or attended private channelings and life readings. Among these are Susan

Batchelder, Benjamin Yates, Toni Maria Pinhiero, Michael Kopel, Adora Dorothy Winquist, Jim Foster, Clayton Bemis, Susan Farley, Pat Gillis, Judy Forrest, Leslie Gabral, Mary Jane Moore, Christine Schreibstein and Beth Sexeny.

My special thanks to Katie Ramaci and her Women of Wisdom group members, to Kenneth and Sandra Frey, to Lucille Kluckas and Christopher Kluckas and the New Jersey group members. These are people whose light shines upon our world and awakens the multitudes and masses. May their light continue to shine ever brighter day by day into eternity.

Last, but not least, I would like to thank Dr. John Alderson, who has been a constant support in the entire process and for his magical healing touch.

Cited Works

Bailey, Alice. *Initiation Human and Solar*. Lucias Publishing Co., 1997.

Bailey, Alice. *Rays and Initiations: A Treatise on the Seven Rays (Rays and the Initiations)*. Lucias Publishing Co., 1960.

Crème, Benjamin. *Maitreya's Mission Vol. I & II*. Share Intl. Foundation. 2002

Crème, Benjamin. *Maitreya's Mission Vol. II*. Share Intl. Foundation.

Crème, Benjamin. *Transmission: A Meditation for the New Age*. Share International Foundation, 2001.

Freke, Timothy and Gandy, Peter. *The Hermetica: The Lost Wisdom of the Pharaohs*.

Doreal. *The Emerald Tablets of Thoth the Atlantean*. Source Books, Inc., 2002

Grattan, Brain. *Mahatma I and II*.

King, Godfrey Ray. *I Am Discourses of St. Germain*.

McClure, Janet. *Sanat Kumara: Training a Planetary Logos (Tools for Transformation)*. Light Technology Publishing, 1990.

Meera, Mother. *Answers Part I*. Mother Meera Publications, Germany 1991.

Peterson, Wayne S. *Extraordinary Times, Extraordinary Beings: Experiences of an American Diplomat with Maitreya and the Masters of Wisdom*.

216

Printz, Thomas. *Memories of Beloved Mary-Mother of Jesus.*

Printz, Thomas. *The Seven Archangels Speak from the Channelings of Geraldine Innocenti.*

Printz, Thomas. *The Seven Mighty Elohim Speak on the Seven Steps to Precipitation.*

Prophet, Mark and Elizabeth Clare. *Lords of the Seven Rays.* Summit University Press, Corwin Springs MT 1986.

Schroeder, Werner. *Man-His Origin, History and Destiny.* Ascended Master Teaching Foundation, 1984.

Szekely, Edmond-Bordeaux. *Essene Gospel of Peace.*

Zargar, Dr. Karim. *Kavir-E-Kimia.* (Original work in Farsi; English translations *Desert of Alchemy, Book of Zohar)*

Information from Organizations or Websites

Karunamayi: www.karunamayi.org

Mother Meera: Send letters in English or German to: Oberdorf 4a, 65599 Dornburg-Thalheim, Germany

Share International Foundation: www.shareintl.org

Summit University Press: www.summituniversitypress.com

St. Germain Foundation: www.stgermainfoundation.org

Women of Wisdom: www.members.aol.com/womnwisdom

Ammachi: www.Amma.org

Universal Seminary — Credit courses in Esoteric Spirituality :www.universalseminary.org

Information on Life Readings

Lord Metatron had instructed me at the turn of the century to offer life readings. He explained that it was time for people who are serious about their spiritual growth to receive assistance from the Masters to connect with their soul lineage and accelerate their growth. Once connected, the flow of energy from the Masters will continue without stopping. Some sensitive souls feel the connection energetically and hear the voices of Masters guiding them directly after their readings.

As I was editing these words, I heard from a woman who had visited her native home in Colombia after her life reading with Archangel Michael. She told me that she felt Archangel Michael's presence with her the entire time on this trip. She taught the Archangel Michael prayer of protection (*Gifts I*) to a child and his mother who had a long journey ahead of them in the dark of night. The child remembered and later taught the prayer to his grandparents and other family members with great joy and ecstasy. She also told me that Lord Metatron would appear to give her instructions regarding her spiritual practice and how to serve others while in Colombia.

Over the years I have seen many lives change when individuals find their Soul Lineage of Light and connect with the Masters or the Angelic Guardians of their respective Rays. These are truly memorable experiences. During one Life Reading, a prominent Ascended Master told a client that she had been his daughter in one of his lifetimes on Earth as a famous king. He gave the king's name and told the client that her mother (the king's wife) had died while giving birth to her. He explained to her that the feeling of abandonment had stayed with her ever since that lifetime because not only did she lose her mother, but also her father — the grief stricken king could not be near her as she reminded him of his loss. The Master offered her healings to remove the pain. My client was able to verify all that information by researching the king's life. She came across her own name, her date and place of birth and her mother's name and details too. The date of her mother's death was the same as her birthdate. This meant that she had indeed lost her life giving birth to her. This verification made the reading all the more real for the client. It moved her to apply the rest of the teachings to her life and to choose greater acceleration of her spiritual growth. In a short time she was led to study many different modalities of healing arts. From them, she created her own blend of spiritual teachings to share with other students of the light. She continued with her life in the outside world with much greater purpose. Her conscious awareness of her Lineage of light and her deep connection with the Master, her own father from another lifetime, gave her greater determination to serve on the path of Light and to help others gain spiritually.

To understand more on the significance of Life Readings, please visit www.NasrinSafai.com and click on Life Readings.

About the Author

Nasrin is been an internationally known Channel of the Ascended Masters and Angelic Beings of Light. In 1999, Lord Metatron requested of Nasrin to conduct channeled life readings to aid those souls who are drawn to find their life's mission and to recall their lineage of Light.

Part of her life's mission is to travel the world anchoring ascension energies of Light at locations on all continent through ceremonies, sacred dances, mantras, prayers and invocations given by The Masters. Nasrin has been a channel for Metatron, Melchizedeck, Archangel Michael, Uriel, Raphael, Jesus, Mother Mary, Buddha, Saint Germain, Quan Yin, Hecate, Athena, Red Feather, and other ascended beings of Light.

She attended Chelsea School of Art in London, received a Bachelors Degree from the University of Decorative Arts in Tehran, a Masters Degree in Environmental Planning from Nottingham University in England and did her Doctoral Studies in the role of women in the development of the third world. She has taught at Harvard University and universities and institutes of higher education around the world. Presently she holds the post of Professor of Esoteric Spirituality at Universal Seminary, where materials from this books are taught for college credit..

Nasrin is the founder of The Foundation for the Attainment of God Unity (FAGU), an educational and wholistic healing non-profit organization which provides classes, workshops, books and support materials for spiritual practice, open to all. All proceeds from the sale of this book support the work of the Masters through FAGU.

Other Books by Nasrin Safai

Gifts From Ascended Beings of Light: Prayers, Meditations, Mantras and Journeys for Soul Growth — Gifts I. Agapi Publishing, 2003.

Gifts of Practical Guidance for Daily Living: Healing, Protection, Manifestation, Enlightemnent — Gifts II. Coming soon from Waves of Bliss Publishing.

Gifts of Wisdom and Truth for the Masters of Light: Tools for Clearing, Release, Abundance and Empowerment — Gifts IV. Coming soon from Waves of Bliss Publishing.

Gifts From Sanat Kumara: The Planetary Logos — Gifts V. Coming soon from Waves of Bliss Publishing.

To purchase a book, visit www.NasrinSafai.com
or email info@WavesOfBliss.com.
For information on making a tax-deductible donation, email info@WavesOfBliss.com

What Is Channeling?

This is a channeled book. The information is channeled from the Higher Realms — the realms of the Ascended Masters and Beings of Light, such as angels, archangels, guides, and guardian angels. These are our elder brothers and sisters who have attained enlightenment and moved to higher dimensions of reality.

What is channeling? The information is transmitted using the channel (in this case, Nasrin) as the vehicle. A channel is a person with great psychic abilities capable of receiving information from the higher realms.

Edgar Cayce (1877-1945), also known as the sleeping prophet and a pioneer in this field, was a trance channel. He channeled information while in an unconscious trance. Other prominent figures in this field are Alice A. Bailey (1880-1947), Madame Helena Blavatsky (Theosophical Society), Louis and Godfre Ray King (*The I AM Discourses of St. Germain*), Mark and Elizabeth Clair Prophet (Summit Light House), Jane Roberts (*The Seth Materals*) and Ruth Montgomery (*Aliens Among Us*). Today the Earth can energetically support channels who remain conscious, so they are aware of what is taking place while it is happening. Nasrin Safai is a conscious channel. She can bring guidance from the Masters, communicate with relatives who have passed over, uncover past lives and see events unfolding from the future. For more information, see wwwNasrinSafai.com.

$18.99
ISBN 0-9767035-0-5
51899>

9 780976 703501